Inclusive Branding

The why and how of a holistic
approach to brands

Klaus Schmidt and Chris Ludlow

First published 2002 by
PALGRAVE MACMILLAN
Houndmills, Basingstoke, Hampshire RG21 6XS and
175 Fifth Avenue, New York, N.Y. 10010
Companies and representatives throughout the world

PALGRAVE MACMILLAN is the global academic imprint of the Palgrave Macmillan
division of St. Martin's Press, LLC and of Palgrave Macmillan Ltd. Macmillan® is a
registered trademark in the United States, United Kingdom and other countries.
Palgrave is a registered trademark in the European Union and other countries.

ISBN 0–333–98079–4 hardback

This book is printed on paper suitable for recycling and made from fully managed and
sustained forest sources.

A catalogue record for this book is available from the British Library.

A catalog record for this book is available from the Library of Congress

Designed and typeset by Curran Publishing Services, Norwich

10 9 8 7 6 5 4 3 2 1
11 10 09 08 07 06 05 04 03 02

Printed and bound in Great Britain by
Creative Print & Design (Wales), Ebbw Vale

Contents

List of figures and tables

Figures

Tables

Acknowledgements

This book could not have been produced without the assistance and cooperation of the authors of the individual case histories. We are indebted to them for the time and trouble they took, whether in writing, sourcing illustrations, checking, proofreading or simply discussing their work and their companies. We also thank Nick Kochan and Helen Triggs for their assistance with texts, and Don Landers at Springetts for special help with Manchester United.

Thanks are also due to Stephen Rutt and Jacky Kippenberger at Palgrave Macmillan. Stephen's encouragement and support made the task of delivering the manuscript almost bearable, and his general advice on many aspects of the book was most gratefully accepted.

We would like especially to thank all those at Henrion Ludlow Schmidt who have participated in many different ways in the creation of the book, and particularly Imke Schiller and Maren Kleinert for their work on the content of charts and diagrams, Helmut Hauke for the appearance of same, and Dan Hiblin for the style of the book, along with the publisher's own designers.

The page from the *Sun*, London, Wednesday 30 January 1991, is © News International Newspapers Limited, London.

The cover of *No Logo* is reproduced by kind permission of Harper-Collins Publishers Ltd. © 2000 Naomi Klein.

The quote on page 55 is from *Built to Last* by James C. Collins and Jerry I. Porras, published by Random House Business Books, reprinted by permission of The Random House Group Ltd.

Foreword

Everybody seems to have an opinion about brands. Brand people – those who earn their livings through promoting or engineering brands – discuss methods, benefits and budgets. Those outside the machinery of brand creation and manipulation – consumers and commentators – are polarized in their views. They seem either to love brands or to loathe them. On the one hand, youth culture demands the ownership and display of 'cool' brands as a mark of status and belonging. On the other hand, anti-capitalist activists cite brands as the cause of all sorts of ills, from third world labour exploitation to political manipulation.

The brands most discussed, praised, vilified or featured in books are global consumer brands; many are American brands in food and clothing. But these days most things – products, services, companies, pop groups, celebrities, charities, nations and even wars – are branded, and they encompass fast-moving consumer goods, through professional services and capital goods, to conglomerates and utilities. These brands exist so that they can compete in a big, bad world, and they need all the help they can get.

But they are not always getting it. What they are often getting are limited and blinkered approaches, where the self-interest of brand advisers precludes a properly inclusive view of what influences brand perceptions and brand development. The world has moved on, but practices for dealing with brands seem stuck in a narrow kind of thinking which admits nothing beyond what is conventionally accepted in branding circles.

However, there are signs that we are nearing the end of the road for such myopic views of what has become a subject of strategic significance, not just for the global mega-brands that are always touted as exemplars, but for all brands.

Inclusive branding is the new (or, in some senses, not so new) paradigm, with its emphasis on the holistic approach. The new thrust will be on mobilization and optimization of all resources to focus on defining and realizing the brand promise, because the universal competition that all brands are facing will dictate that.

The world is experiencing its third industrial revolution. The first was production driven. The second was market driven. The third is knowledge driven. Production itself is becoming a matter of knowledge-based sourcing, and marketing is being driven by ever more detailed knowledge of customers, whose buying decisions are increasingly centred on their knowledge, or perceptions, of brands.

In this new era, brands will rule as never before. But the already overcrowded and unreasonably competitive conditions will change ever faster. The audience, especially, will change. It will become even more fragmented and demanding, with access to vastly more knowledge. The implications for how brands will be developed and managed are dramatic.

These trends have been detectable for some time, and in 1989 I initiated a series of pan-European studies called 'Corporate Identity in a Multicultural Marketplace', which showed the urgent need for a more comprehensive approach. Subsequently, I defined and developed the concept of the 'holistic approach', in response to the needs which were expressed, and in the light of our own client experiences with large international organizations. At that time, there were no existing tools, methodologies or processes even to address, never mind exploit, global complexities in competition, consolidation, cultural differences, taste, personal attitudes and values, technological challenges, and the alarmingly accelerative speed of change. This was partly due to the fact that cooperation between disciplines, for example marketing and human resources, just did not exist. There was widespread 'silo thinking', which was reflected in corporate structures.

Acceptance of the 'holistic' idea grew slowly but surely. We pioneered it through working with a number of enlightened clients, achieving revelatory results. In 1994, I wrote the first book on the subject, and now many other consultancies and 'agencies' claim to have a 'holistic approach', or to be holistic in some other way, although none has the range and depth of methods and tools which we have developed over the years.

Our main purpose in this book is to demonstrate what we have been practising and preaching for the past decade and more: that universal competition and global complexity can only be faced, and turned to competitive advantage, through an approach to brands that includes all the 'dimensions', both external and internal, that are relevant to building them and to how they are perceived. Indeed, this will become the only approach in future, for it is the only one which effectively takes on board economic, organizational and human realities.

The book combines background, theory and practice. The holistic approach is explained in detail, and timely reasons are given as to why it is so relevant now – and in the foreseeable future. It is also demonstrated why the holistic approach remains unique in its concept, that it is not just a new label for an old offer, but a management tool, a way to manage a brand, an organization, a company. Its usefulness and its value, ten years after its introduction, are now of even greater consequence.

The examples in the second part of the book give extensive and topical insights from within all sorts of significant organizations that are grappling with the daily realities of holistic branding, although they might not all call it such. The message comes across loud and clear: branding is always a key element of corporate strategy, often the leading element, and increasingly the conceptual basis.

Brands are at a crossroads. They are on the front page of the *Financial Times* and on the lips of millions. The subject is discussed in boardrooms and brands appear as assets on the balance sheet. They are so pervasive that popular voices have even been raised in anger against their power. No longer a question of simple external marketing support, they have burst into the arena of corporate and business strategy and are penetrating the enclaves of human resource strategies, environmental policies, production quality, service standards and (somewhat controversially) the balance sheet.

If brands have reached this level of ubiquity and potential, then the signals are clear: brands demand strategic management, led from the very top. And that should include all the aspects that affect them, and through which they can be communicated. This is an irresistible proposition for inclusive branding through the holistic approach.

Dr Klaus Schmidt
London, 2002

Chapter 1
Inclusive Branding: Roots and Reasons

From cattle to Coke

Brands are the basis of choice. They encapsulate the reasons and emotions that cause us to buy one thing rather than something else. Brands add value to products, services and companies, for the benefit of all stakeholders. Vast sums of money and effort are expended on the creation, development and promotion of brands. And the pace is quickening, indicative of the increasing importance of brands in our consumer society. Brands also have a history, which helps us to understand their power, their potential, and the context for the genesis of inclusive branding.

Although conventional wisdom sometimes states that brands add an emotional pull to rational choices, this is only part of the story. A brand's original role was only to identify, as with herds of cattle in the Wild West. Later, brands were applied to products to trigger or aid recall at the vital moment when a buying choice was made. The mental picture, or 'image', at the point of recall could have been influenced by any one, or any combination, of a number of points, such as prior experience of a product or service, the advertising campaign, the behaviour of a salesperson, or the pack design. Perceptions could also have been influenced, at this early stage, by knowledge of who or what stood behind the brand, and what their reputations were.

Originally, 'brand' applied specifically to the name of whatever was identified, but it was soon recognized that emotional appeal could be added through visual style and brand communications. In this way, from the name itself to the packs, bill boards and advertising (not to mention the products themselves, which were not seen as an element of branding, only as the thing to be sold), brands could be created to address specific target markets and market segments. So, as societies developed and lifestyle distinctions became more and more individually identifiable, brands could be tuned to appeal to specific purchasing groups. A history of brands does, indeed, resemble a social history, so immediate are the responses to fashions, tastes, needs and values. So, early in the history of branding, the vital need to understand the customer was established.

That a brand was something that could be tagged onto an otherwise generic product or a commodity, thereby creating difference, appeal and value, was an early idea and one that has persisted into present times. This eventually led to misleading attempts to assign monetary values to brands. Their accuracy and credibility, are neatly summed up by two widely differing findings about the value of Coca-Cola's brand in 2001.

Brand equity, Coca-Cola, 2001	
AC Nielsen	*Interbrand*
$ 15 billion	$ 68.945 billion
Source: www.acnielsen.com	

Brands are an old idea with a long history. The real impetus for their development was the need to sell the products of industry, but the question of who stood behind brands was eventually to come to the fore.

'Brand' or 'corporate identity'?

Another important strand in the general history of brands is the phenomenon and discipline of 'corporate identity', which was perceived differently in, for example, the United States, the UK and Germany, but which has converged with old-style branding.

Before the middle of the 1990s, the term 'brand' was mainly confined to consumer goods and specific products and services. Confectionery products, tobacco goods, electrical appliances, cars and furniture were

Mars is the product brand, but also the company behind it

branded, and some brands were also the companies that made the products, like Coca-Cola or Mars.

Companies who stood behind the products were often different from the products themselves in that they were more likely to have a 'corporate identity' than a 'brand'. Corporate identity was usually dealt with separately from brands, and usually, in the United States and the UK, by design-driven, so-called corporate identity consultants. In Germany, corporate identity was already seen as a broader issue involving elements of culture and values. In all areas, it was considered a longer-term issue than branding and included complexities such as corporate naming and graphics systems for subsidiaries or divisions, 'endorsement' of brands by the corporate signature or expression of hierarchies and interrelationships, as well as the basic elements such as logotypes, symbols, colours and type styles. Where corporate identity started from a root of visual coordination, it had also come to include matters of worldwide implementation and design management, but most importantly, it also naturally came to include some of the internal aspects which the word 'identity' so clearly implies.

For identity is a matter of self-awareness as well as the external expression of characteristics. In taking account of this, corporate identity became concerned with the basic purpose of organizations. Even when corporate identity was only considered as a purely visual discipline, the initial investigation and briefing process demanded answers to radical questions about a company's direction. This probing for answers to basic questions often had a catalytic effect on organizations, and presented a very direct route into the area of corporate strategy.

Corporate identity, as a concept, has a very long and distinguished history. Its root is quite separate from that of branding. You can trace it back to ancient times, when tribes, religions and civilizations used distinctive insignia and dress to identify themselves. Its modern development dates from early industrialization when companies, as highly organized units, began to

3

Classic corporate identities of large international organizations

compete with each other and sought differentiation. The coordinated design that was one element of identity also extended in some cases from stationery to factories, from office interiors to signs, and from uniforms to products. The example of IBM employing various world-class designers and architects in the post-war years comes to mind. This scheme – and other trailblazers such as Olivetti and AEG – were very complete expressions of corporate philosophy and strategy, led from the very top of the respective organizations.

By the early 1990s many people, including the general public in the UK, felt that some of the results of so-called corporate identity exercises in the recent past were banal in the extreme, and lacking the authentic qualities displayed by IBM, for example. When British Telecom was transformed into BT, with its 'piper' symbol, voices were raised in derision about the result, and in disgust about the cost, partly because the latter was routinely overstated by the media. Much more recently, British Airways was caught in the same trap, but in their case it was really clear that too much attention had

AEG's comprehensive approach to visual coordination is one of
the earliest examples, and is considered pioneering

been paid to external gloss, which created a mismatch with reality. The general opinion was that the money could have been better spent on staff training or service improvements. The scheme was abandoned, at great cost, having become extremely unpopular because of its seemingly unpatriotic abandonment of the Union flag. In truth, it could never have worked as it betrayed the first principles of identification – that consistency creates recognizability.

But these high-profile problems, which did much

The *Sun* newspaper ridiculed the BT piper on
its introduction in 1991, on the back of a wave
of criticism

damage to the image of image-building, exposed the design-centric practice of much of the corporate identity 'industry', including consultants and their client counterparts. Nobody in their right mind would deny the importance of a first, visual impression, but surely there must be more to it than that. The restyle of Aeroflot's brand, for example, could in no way itself reverse the reputation built up by decades of horror stories.

Aside from corporate identity, other ideas, concepts and methods to give substance to a corporate or brand image were being put forward by various gurus and practitioners. Claims of effectiveness were made for corporate culture development, internal communications, vision, mission and values development, training programmes and so on, all offering their own distinctive, but limited, approaches. Although none of them was the total solution that their individual proponents suggested, most of them did form part of the picture. The recognition of culture, in particular, as a dimension of communications was very welcome. But others, such as the often hollow and irrelevant vision, mission and values (VMV) statement were, when created in a vacuum, worse than useless. In fact the VMV, which is the vital core of a brand, has hardly recovered from the reputation it gained for vagueness and irrelevance.

So 'corporate identity', although clearly possessing huge potential, was generally still at an uneven stage of development, and was being claimed by various disciplines. It was as though all the pieces were there, but not the overall picture.

The best of both worlds

Around the mid-1990s those who dealt in the area of brands began to talk about, and promote, ideas such as 'delivering the brand promise' and 'living the brand'. These showed that their thinking was progressing in the direction of the substance behind the brand, which meant that the seemingly independent courses of corporate identity and branding were headed towards the same territory. The basic principle which both now embraced was that creation of a brand, an identity, should not be a superficial exercise led by external impressions alone, but must be an expression of something substantial, something rooted in reality, with real relevance to all stakeholders, staff and customers.

The word 'brand' began its ascendancy to general usage and to the boardroom. But the principles of corporate identity were to be the building blocks for the future development of brand thinking and practice, from single consumer product brands to complex corporate brands and brand hierarchies.

Some individual disciplines were very defensive about these developments, particularly advertising, which was (and is) under threat anyway. Advertising was far too simple a response to the problems of many a brand. Clients were rebelling against high charges for media space and creative services, and some agencies had responded by transforming themselves into broad-based marketing services or communications groups. 'One-stop shop' was the new idea, followed more recently by 'integrated communications'. To integrate communications 'above and below the line' is, of course, no bad idea, and is more likely to create synergies than are uncoordinated activities. But it is totally limited by its component parts, which make it merely an assembly of conventional approaches and measures.

All such specific, narrow approaches are, of course, to some degree institutionalized, and therefore resistant to new thinking and radical change. Corporate structures, often plagued with silo mentalities, reflect the specialisms of corporate advisers (or maybe the other way round), and so it is relatively easy to carry on with the old ways in a kind of narrow, two-way road between client and adviser or agency. On the client side, the marketing department has its director, its managers, its support staff, its offices, its strategy, its annual budget, and perhaps the responsible board member behind it. On the other side are the advertising agency, the PR agency, the design group and so on. The human resources department similarly has its own compartmentalized structure and advisers, as have production, distribution and so on. This is a recipe for blinkered thinking and continuity, not for imaginative, broad rethinking of roles, responsibilities and ways in which to respond to the challenges of a world transforming in front of our eyes.

So 'corporate identity' has become 'branding', but the meaning and relevance of the latter has been transformed in the process. Old, narrow ways of developing and managing brands will not do: the world is too complex and fast-changing.

Brand environment: the world

If there is one thing that characterizes the world of the twenty-first century, it must be change. Evolutionary or revolutionary, technological or cultural, change proceeds in all things, the common denominator being that the pace seems to be quickening on an exponential basis. Chaos seems to threaten.

Within this overall picture, there are many detail variations and inconsistencies. Attitudes and value systems lag behind technology, which always seems to be stretching our ability to cope with it. Organizational change is more or less constant, and fashion responds to its own timetable. Predicting change is a constant preoccupation, yet it regularly catches us out, and brands are especially sensitive to change.

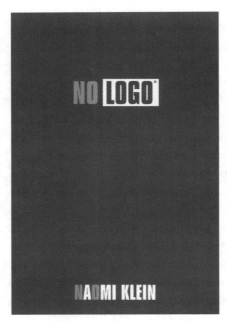

Naomi Klein's seminal book *No Logo* touched a nerve in describing the effects of powerful global brands

Internationalization and globalization have been proceeding for decades, in some industries faster than in others, but usually driven by the need for larger markets and lower production costs. The subject of global brands themselves is discussed in greater detail in Chapter 3, but suffice to say here that differing global and local requirements, cultures and communications create tensions to challenge the most professional brand management systems. Even Douglas Daft, CEO of the mighty Coca-Cola, has admitted that 'we probably did not under-stand the world as well as we thought we did', and has embarked on a major rethink of the global/local balance.

Brands have also come under fire. Global consumer brands' influence and activities have been subjected to intense scrutiny, catching some on the hop. Responses to environmental issues, mishaps, and corporate behaviour in third-world countries have often been the benchmarks by which they have been popularly judged. This powerful public awareness took many by surprise, and some corporate brands, in particular, were clumsy in their responses, learning slowly that their behaviour was crucial to their standing and long-term success.

Competition has become more intense than could have been

Invensys
Avensis
Aventis
Aviva
Arriva
Avaya

Interchangeable names seem to be on the increase. Are they really a sound basis for identification and differentiation?

thought possible, in many business areas. Resulting cost pressures mean that companies must now identify more effective ways to achieve profile and differentiation. This is one reason why classical advertising has been hit so hard: it has become so enormously and indulgently expensive.

Consolidation is another trend that is fuelled by cost pressures and that has enormous implications for brands. When companies merge, naming is an issue, and existing corporate brands can sink without trace. You may not know who Aventis is, but you possibly still remember Hoechst and Rhône-Poulenc. Aventis (not Avensis; that's a Toyota car!) is the nondescript name for the combined organization. So when do you really need a new name, and when should you retain the old ones?

Homogenization of products and services means that they cannot be used as an obvious and secure basis for differentiation or competitive advantage any more. Convergence of technologies in design and production in, for example, the car industry has led to the situation where the performance and tactile quality of a Volkswagen is now hardly inferior to that of a comparable BMW. Computer hardware, too, has virtually become a commodity, and technical advances merely give a temporary lead before the copy-cats catch up. All the same, those in the race must continue to innovate, or drop out completely. There is a temptation to see brands as the holy grail in such difficult circumstances, but simple, superficial branding activities will not have a significant or lasting effect.

Volkswagen Passat

BMW 5-series

Lastly, customer expectations have reached dizzy heights. Your customers are aware of the performance and style of your products and services, and of their strengths and weaknesses in relation to those of your competitors. They know your reputation for after-sales service and how you deal with complaints. They want to know if the environmental performance of your company accords with their own values, and if you test your products on animals. They are also shareholders and expect decent returns, and are interested in how you treat your employees. If you live up to their expectations, you may be rewarded with a degree of loyalty. If not, you will not survive.

The global environment within which brands must survive is demanding, unforgiving and always changing. The challenges and opportunities this presents for brands must be faced on their own terms.

Lessons from real life

Later on, we present in-depth cases which describe how particular brands have been developed and managed, often in the face of difficult circumstances. Even cursory observation of some brands is enough to provide overwhelming evidence that organizations succeed when their brands are vision-led and implemented through an active and consistent strategy which embraces and guides all aspects of the business. There is equal evidence that the reverse is true: when brands are considered as an add-on for short-term tactical advantage, or when key aspects of the business do not align with brand values, success is threatened, or disasters occur.

Having ignored its customers' preferences for far too long, apart from assuming their eternal loyalty and their eager willingness not to pay by credit card, Marks and Spencer fell off the edge of a cliff. Sales plummeted, shareholders were dismayed, the firm's reputation was in tatters. Even the legendary quality of 'St Michael' underwear and socks was called into question. This dramatic failure was front-page and prime-time-television news, and the heads of top management rolled and continue to roll from time to time.

Less than one year after this debacle, and with no better news on the horizon, Marks and Spencer carried out a 'rebranding' programme: a new logotype, a fresher green colour for the classic carrier bag and so on. Nobody noticed, nobody cared. Why should they? Nothing had really changed, and one year later the problems continued, completely unaffected by this superficial tinkering. Staff and customer cynicism had taken up residence.

British Airways' difficulties have already been mentioned. Contrast their approach with that of easyJet, a UK budget airline. EasyJet has a clear mission to provide inexpensive, fuss-free flights. The airline makes a strong expression of the whole 'big idea' through every aspect of its activities: name, fares, visual impression, booking systems and on-board service. Other easyGroup brands such as easyCar, easyInternetCafé, easyValue, easyMoney and easy.com all continue the theme. Of course, the charismatic Stelios Haji-Ioannou, owner of easyJet, is the principal source of the company's vision, direction and energy, although the brand does not seem to be as dependent on him as Virgin is on Richard Branson. In fact, he relinquished overall control without any detriment to the brands. EasyJet's financial results, as well as its growth through acquisition, speak for the effectiveness of its brand-led corporate strategy.

American brands usually top global league tables and Coca-Cola, despite its difficulties, still regularly emerges as number one. But there have been notable problems at some US companies. Many forget that IBM was in severe difficulties ten years ago, when a too-rigid, institutionalized interpretation of the famed 'Basic Beliefs' – the heart of the IBM brand – combined with hubris on a grand scale. Most people remember the 'nobody was ever sacked for buying IBM' years. This presumption and remoteness from reality caused IBM to lose touch with customers, lose business and then lose confidence in its own abilities to right the situation. Because IBM had looked after its people, in line with one of the 'Basic Beliefs', pruning the workforce was delayed. When it was no longer possible to delay further, the process was so painful that it shook IBM to its roots. From this position, it was forced to take a radical view and rebuild the brand based on customer focus and flexibility. In this case, the guiding vision had been allowed to ossify, leading the brand in an irrelevant direction. Today's IBM is a different animal: responsive, proactive and successful.

The German brands most often quoted as exemplary are those of cars, but they are not infallible. Witness the case of the Porsche Boxster, which is an example of how lack of understanding of customers, as expressed through the product, can create alienation within the brand. The Boxster was originally launched as a highly original, entry-level product. When a new 911 (Porsche's traditional premium model) was subsequently introduced, the front light units from the Boxster were used for the new car.

Result: lack of differentiation of the more expensive car, betrayal of Porsche's long-standing brand values – and bemused customers. Rather too late, modifications were put in hand.

In general, of course, German cars partly created, and now benefit from, associations with quality engineering. Mercedes-Benz, surely the premier global automotive brand, is one of our case histories. The story of Müller yoghurt in the UK demonstrates that the German consistency and thoroughness of approach can be just as powerful in other sectors. Müller, a Bavarian producer of dairy products, entered the UK market in 1987 by importing its 'Fruit Corner' product. Both name (very German, with its umlauts) and product (leading British competitors at the time said it would never take off) were unpromising. But Müller stuck to its guns, aligning product, promotion, distribution and every other business aspect to support its vision. By 1992, Müller had enough proof of success to build and open its own production facility in a prime dairy area of England. Müller is now the leading yoghurt brand in Britain. That success is not based on the name, but on consistency of strategic concept, operation, expression and delivery of brand values, which the name now conveys.

Moben is a British furniture company. It decided to call itself 'Möben', a quick but deceitful way of borrowing the German reputation for quality for itself. Such a difference between reality and desired effect is not sustainable, and prejudices target audiences.

Perhaps the word itself has German associations, but to add the umlaut could be considered the 'last straw' in attempting to warp reality.

Reality caught up with Moben, for there was an open discussion of their actions and motives in the marketing press at the time. Someone with experience of the company wrote about the delays, inconvenience and unprofessionalism displayed by Moben, in contrast to their aspired-to teutonic values. Moben's branding actions illustrate, in an extreme form, that dissonances between brand dimensions only create confusion, or worse.

Which brings us to a branding enigma: Ford. Ford is the world's second-largest car manufacturer, as well as a major financial services provider in its own right. The company has latterly become a collector of brands, most of which are doing quite nicely, thank you. Jaguar, Land-Rover, Aston-Martin and Volvo all seem healthy, or potentially so. Ford's ownership of Jaguar, for example, has done the 'cat' no harm at all, since it had the good sense to keep the Coventry firm at arm's length, pouring in investment, but largely preserving the spirit of the cars. But the core Ford brand is not in such good shape everywhere in the world.

The brand did well in the United States, but in Europe it was a poor performer, despite products highly praised by road testers. Financially speaking, that position is currently reversed, but there is the distinct impression that Ford does not know what it stands for, nor where it's going. Its traditional, once-famous marketing skills seem inadequate, and the antiquated internal mindset of 'research customers – design product – manufacture – sell' still prevails. In this case, it is the organization and culture that are the suspected culprits, and no amount of superficial brand first-aid will cure the patient. Ford needs to return to first principles to sort out its vision for the brand, then align all of its processes and products. It will be a long job, but there is evidence that the company is tackling it.

It is obvious that superficially applied branding measures are not a panacea, and can even be harmful. However, the potential of strategically considered holistic brands as strategic driving forces, and subsequently as success factors, is immense.

Research meets experience

Between 1989 and 1996, we carried out through MORI (London-based, internationally known research agency Market and Opinion Research International) a series of studies which we called 'Corporate Identity in a Multicultural Marketplace'. The marketplace in question was Europe – a microcosm of the globe – and we wanted to cast light on some aspects of our experience, to understand our own market better, and to use the results in formulating a new approach, methods and tools.

The experience that had alerted us to the need for a more inclusive approach had been gained on large, global projects for clients such as

Coopers & Lybrand, KLM and Mitsubishi Motors. Not only were these extremely complex, but the cultural differences encountered cried out for a systematic approach, which would optimize the inherent potential and, in doing so, reduce the 'frictional losses'. Closer to home, the issue of European integration was a prime concern (it still is, of course) and cultural differences were marked, so we decided to carry out research in nine European countries. The sample was composed of top managers responsible for corporate identity in the top 100 or 500 companies in each country.

Most of the issues we summarize later in this chapter were acknowledged as present and valid even then, but hardly any of the managers to whom MORI spoke had any idea of what could actually be done to address them. There was a complete absence of method, or structure. Then, as is still sometimes the case, responsibility for the overall picture just seemed to slip down the gaps between different corporate functions or departments. Yes, they said, values were influential on the perceived corporate image, but values were 'done' by human resources; environmental incidents were a major concern for the corporate profile, but they were handled by facilities management, production or corporate affairs; staff behaviour was affecting customer attitudes, but that was the concern of customer relations. And so on, and so on. It was the silo mentality we mentioned earlier.

The studies also confirmed our experience in other ways. For example, understanding of corporate identity was very varied throughout the different countries, as were perceptions of its benefits, the greatest differences being between the UK and Germany. Characteristically, corporate identity in the UK was seen as primarily an external, visual matter. In Germany it was more comprehensive, embracing internal and external aspects. And although cultural differences were acknowledged as highly problematical, no way was seen to deal with them, at least in this context.

Meanwhile, out there, marketing directors and others were conceiving original brand positionings and strategies, producing award-winning creative executions and launching sparkling 'corporate identities', only to see product, service delivery or corporate behaviour

Pan-European research

The holistic approach to branding was strongly influenced by research we commissioned from MORI at intervals between 1989 and 1996. These tables show a small sample of the results, which indicate not only the differences between European markets, but also the perceived complexities of the subject. The study also established the importance of branding in the context of globalization.

How, briefly, would you define corporate identity?

	Total %	Britain %	France %	Germany %	Scandi-navia %	Austria %	Benelux %	Portugal %
Public image/ external projection	57	**73**	57	**61**	40	**67**	60	40
Visual presentation/ logo	16	**27**	10	13	20	7	7	20
Expression of culture/values	13	**23**	3	**26**	10	13	0	0
Internal projection	11	7	3	**29**	7	**20**	7	7
Product/brand support	11	17	**20**	3	7	7	**20**	0
Behaviour of staff/company personality	10	7	0	**23**	0	**20**	27	7
Company philosophy/ how company sees itself	7	0	0	16	3	**27**	0	7

What do you see as the benefits of a strong corporate identity?

	Total	Britain	France	Germany	Scandi-navia	Austria	Benelux	Portugal
	%	%	%	%	%	%	%	%
Public profile/ recognition	46	53	23	**68**	40	**80**	27	27
Attracts customers/ helps customer relations	20	**30**	10	3	**37**	0	**33**	33
Product/ brand support	19	**30**	17	0	**30**	13	7	33
Visual presentation/ unity	15	10	7	10	3	**27**	**27**	53
Financial advantages/ confidence among financial community	13	20	**23**	6	7	7	7	20
Expresses culture/values	11	**30**	3	3	10	7	13	13
Staff motivation	11	10	3	**23**	0	**27**	0	20
Support for advertising	7	13	3	0	3	0	13	**27**

How important a role would you say corporate identity has in supporting globalization and internationalization in general?

	Total	Britain	France	Germany	Scandi-navia	Austria	Benelux	Portugal
	%	%	%	%	%	%	%	%
Very important	60	60	53	77	50	80	33	67
Fairly important	25	30	27	23	23	13	40	13
Not very/not at all important	12	3	10	0	10	7	7	13

fail to support (or even move in a contrary direction to) the desired target, and fail to deliver the brand promise. They also witnessed advertising and marketing campaigns failing to cross national boundaries, undermining attempts to internationalize or globalize communications.

The waste of effort, and therefore money, was the most obvious result of this kind of blinkered thought and action. High on the list also was the effect on employees of conflicting signals. What were they supposed to think if internal memos contradicted what they saw in their companies' consumer advertising campaigns? What were they supposed to do if the internal culture went counter to publicly stated aims? How were they to cope with instructions from remote head offices that dictated content and style that was meaningless (or worse) in the context of their own cultures? Externally, how were customers to understand poor after-sales service, which totally failed to support an excellent product? And how was the community living next to a polluting chemical plant expected to react to a corporate advertising campaign for the same company, featuring green fields and smiling children?

The need for a broad, comprehensive, approach thus seemed clear to us even then. Nowhere was there a convincing model, or a methodology that acknowledged the reality of the global context and broke free from biased notions of brand development.

The case for a new approach

Thus our own experience, together with the knowledge gained through the studies (and confirmed by what was happening all around us), pushed us to the inescapable conclusion that a new approach was needed. Here are the reasons summarized:

- The world is entering a new knowledge-driven era, in which brands will be a more powerful and decisive influence on corporate or business success than ever before.
- Brands (in which term we have subsumed 'corporate identity') are potentially too valuable to entrust to narrow disciplines such as advertising, which tend to perpetuate their own restricted approaches.

- The world is already too complex and too fast-changing for simple, superficial approaches, which don't allow a full response to new challenges, let alone advantage to be taken of them.
- Competition has been unreasonable for some time and is getting more and more intense.
- Consolidation means having to cope with the integration of internal cultures and with external identification.
- Globalization introduces further cultural and logistics dimensions as added layers of complexity.
- Products and services are becoming more and more alike, with fewer possibilities for differentiation.
- Customers want to know all about a brand from all sides: where it comes from, who makes it, what it does for them, and whether it wreaks havoc on the environment or their community.
- There is a crushing weight of evidence that shows convincingly that brand – and therefore corporate – success depends on alignment of all brand experiences with a relevant, motivating and powerful vision.

What was needed was an inclusive perspective, and a process, which would enable an organization to identify and pinpoint those factors or drivers – across a whole spectrum of relevant dimensions – that influenced its identity or its brand, and to quantify their effects; then, in an involving and participatory way, to set a guiding vision and goals. Finally, the organization needed to return to each dimension in turn to devise and implement ways and means to bring the vision to life, using all available resources. This, in essence, is the basis of our holistic approach to brands and branding.

Chapter 2
Vision into Reality

The holistic approach

The holistic approach is the embodiment of inclusive branding. It was created as a positive response to our experience on global projects over many years, to the results of our 'Corporate Identity in a Multicultural Marketplace' studies, and to knowledge of changing world market conditions. It consists of a structure model and a process. These are described here in turn: first, the model and its constituent parts including the holistic positioning and the dimensions; then, the process.

The holistic brand model

The structure model expresses the six interdependent dimensions of a holistic brand. At its core is a holistic brand positioning, which is influenced by, and implemented through, the six dimensions. The structure enables accurate diagnosis of causes and effects, both in establishing the status quo and in envisaging the future. It is this which makes the holistic approach to branding so complete and practical and so different from piecemeal approaches.

The holistic positioning

The holistic positioning is a six-dimensional description of how the organization or brand sees and understands itself, and of how it is seen and understood by others. It can be applied to a current or to an aspirational situation.

The word 'positioning' is normally used in a marketing context to denote the distinctive market position which a brand has, or wishes to have,

The holistic brand model includes all the dimensions of which a brand consists, allowing interrelated perceptions and influences to be identified and managed

in relation to its competition. This is usually measured by market research and plotted on 'maps' which have pairs of relevant, opposing axes. Although relatively crude, this is still a relevant measure within the market dimension, but in holistic terms it is one-dimensional, and therefore only a part of the whole picture. The drivers of the holistic positioning are the vision, mission and values of the brand or organization, together with a set of 'differentiation factors'. Because the term 'vision, mission and values' is so widely and variously used, we need to record our own definition, as follows:

Vision: an aspirational statement of brand or corporate intent.

Mission: the main ways by which the intent will be pursued.

Values: attributes of the brand or corporate ethos, which will shape both individual and corporate attitudes and behaviour.

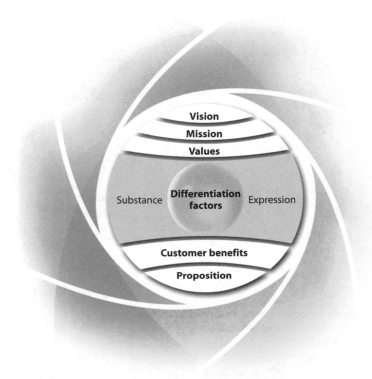

The holistic positioning sits at the core of the holistic brand model.
It is influenced by, and influences, the six dimensions

These are Anglo-Saxon definitions. In Germany, for example, they might refer to a 'Leitbild' (theme) rather than a vision, but the idea is similar. We must be aware, however, that cultural differences are of major concern in such a 'soft' area.

The differentiation factors sum up the main points of difference between 'our' brand or company and others. They may be derived from aspects of resources, competences, qualities, or even values. They are accompanied by a range of essential supporting factors grouped under two headings, 'substance' and 'expression', which can also be seen as objective and subjective differentiation criteria. 'Substance' deals with those objective realities that must be present if the brand is to deliver its promise. 'Expression' is concerned with the subjective associations and intangibles that convey the character of the brand. From these are drawn the customer benefits, which are the prerequisites of the final element, the brand proposition.

The holistic positioning is therefore an all-embracing description of a brand's vision, mission and values, its differentiation factors in substance and expression, along with its transparently derived customer benefits and summary proposition.

The six dimensions

The six dimensions reflect areas of operational relevance. Although explained individually here, they are to be seen as parts of an interdependent whole, never as truly separate. The dimensions are:

- Culture
- Behaviour
- Products and services
- Markets and customers
- Design
- Communications.

The entry point to a branding problem or project can be through any one, or any combination, of the dimensions, according to where the problem, or the opportunity, is considered to be.

Culture

Culture can be considered the pivotal point of many branding projects, in that the internal culture of the organization is a predominant determining factor. It can also be considered as a basic influence on attitudes and behaviour, as well as a communications medium in its own right. Culture is at the core of a brand's positioning and expression.

We include in the culture dimension all of those aspects that an organization uses, consciously or unconsciously, to prescribe its culture. These include, for example, leadership style, history, 'rituals', environment

Culture

Substance

History
Values
Principles
Attitudes
Atmosphere

Expression

Flexible
Open
Cooperative
Customer-focused
Pro-active

and precedent. We also include the definition of the 'atmosphere' of an organization which, of course, influences, and is influenced by, the internal behaviours. Within this fall attitudes, expectations, concerns and other expressions of a typical, distinctive and describable culture.

The national or regional cultures within which an organization must operate can be considered as distinct from corporate culture, although these external cultures certainly influence internal cultures. A global brand must be acceptable in and adaptable to all cultural environments in which it operates. Influences will include history, arts, political situation and many other factors.

A positive culture – flexible and entrepreneurial, for example – is a major success factor which creates a virtuous circle of motivation and successful results. A negative culture, on the other hand, can be a real hindrance to the achievement of corporate goals, as can the mismatch of different cultures. This can happen at a merger or acquisition, or in different subsidiaries or divisions of one organization. Of those mergers that fail, the majority do so because of cultural incompatibilities, and many merged organizations never realize their full potential, for the same reason. A forward-looking, unified culture that distils the spirit of the merger and encourages buy-in is an absolute prerequisite.

Different cultures will often be present in the various national subsidiaries of an international organization, and although these can create communicative and operational problems at various levels, they can also bring benefits if harnessed for the corporate good. Cross-border mergers and acquisitions, which compound these factors, are therefore particularly fraught with cultural difficulties as well as, of course, potential.

Industries and business areas also have their own individual cultures.

One of the biggest differences is between fast-moving consumer goods (FMCG) and business-to-business (B2B), the former based on a numerically large but relatively remote customer base, the latter on closer contact with fewer customers. In addition, the culture of professional services organizations, such as law firms, is very different from that of industrial concerns.

In general, internal culture is the most deep-rooted and long-term dimension of branding. It is also the most misunderstood and neglected area. Holistic branding offers an approach to culture analysis and development which respects the role of culture in shaping and fulfilling the brand promise.

Behaviour

Behaviour is partly a result of cultural influences, but can also be led by other factors. We define behaviour within holistic branding as both individual and corporate behaviour. It can clearly have enormous effects internally and externally, both in immediate customer contact with a brand and over the long-term shaping of reputations.

Service industries provide the most obvious illustrations of individual behaviour in action. The behaviour of an airline stewardess, for example, can have a greater impact (positive or negative) on a passenger's perceptions of the airline than a costly corporate advertisement. A salesperson's attitude in a car showroom can make or break a sale, and can also leave a lasting impression of a manufacturer's attitude to its potential customers. A shop assistant's handling of a customer complaint can either compound the problem, or turn it into an opportunity to create an ongoing relationship.

Corporately, behaviour towards the environment, local communities, employees and action groups can all confirm, or deny, the

Behaviour

Substance
Employment policies
Rewards and sanctions
Training
Operational standards
Environmental policies

Expression
Professional
Efficient
Responsive
Entrepreneurial
Socially responsible

image attributes which have been carefully built up through expensive, classical communications. Inconsistency in corporate behaviour is a most destructive influence. Conversely, companies that have built a reputation for positive behaviour are most likely to survive, or even benefit from, the disasters that can occur from time to time.

Inconsistency between behaviour and other messages received from an organization is also very damaging. Launching a new visual identity against a background of industrial relations intransigence is going to affect internal morale as well as external credibility. Running a 'green' corporate advertising campaign while polluting the local river is guaranteed to produce cynicism and anger. These examples seem blindingly obvious in terms of cause and effect, yet such situations continue to occur because of the lack of coherent strategies or responsibilities. Individual and corporate behaviour must therefore be seen as a most important dimension of branding and identity, and any means of influencing it must be grasped and put into effect.

For individual behaviour, specific standards can be formulated and applied, for example in customer service. Culture may form the basis for behaviour, but standards guarantee delivery of the brand promise. Operational standards must reinforce values, and vice versa, and all must reflect the brand or identity positioning.

For corporate behaviour, the mechanism must deal with short-term issues within a framework of long-term consistency, all of which must be based on a holistic brand positioning.

Products and services

The products and services of successful companies are totally aligned with their brand visions and values. In some cases, it is difficult to say whether the products sprang from the values, or the values were built around the product, but in the best examples they form a self-reinforcing continuity which acts as a most convincing long-term basis for a brand or identity. In certain areas – automobiles is the most obvious – the product is even dominant, and its styling overtly expresses the brand values which are also embodied in all sorts of recognizable elements, from the overall shape to the details of texture and feel of switches and upholstery.

Recognizability and long-term brand value depend therefore on a product strategy that embraces the brand or corporate positioning. And the strategy will also define the approach to aspects such as ergonomics and safety, for example, through which corporate attitudes to users are expressed.

The convergence in the characteristics of products and services has led to a general consensus that brands can add the distinctiveness which is missing from a product or service itself. To an extent, this is true. But the product must align, or be capable of alignment, with brand values or specific claims, and the stronger the alignment, the stronger the brand.

Similarly with product benefits: the product should yield benefits which support the brand positioning. This seems an obvious proposition, but there are many examples of products which lack the appropriate benefits. They therefore create doubts about the brand promise and tend to destroy credibility in the minds of consumers. This once again demonstrates the interdependence of all the dimensions.

Products & services

Substance
Quality
Service standards
Performance
Research and development
Range

Expression
Appealing
Modern
Individual
Distinctive
User-friendly

Services, or more precisely the delivery of services, are more directly influenced by cultural and behavioural factors. In fact, many services are totally defined by how they are delivered. It is in service delivery, which is so highly dependent on individual motivation and attitudes, that holistic branding is so effective, even essential. It provides the basic preconditioning, as well as the specific operational standards, that help to ensure that delivery – one of the final links in the chain – supports the brand positioning and fulfils the brand promise.

Markets and customers

The external market defines the company or the brand to a large extent: no

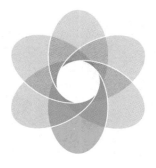

Markets & customers

Substance
Market position
Segmentation
Marketing strategies
Customer profile
Competitors

Expression
Competitive
Leading edge
Charismatic
Sympathetic
Dynamic

company or brand exists in a vacuum. The market, and the organization's response to it, forms the content of perhaps the most complex of our six dimensions. It is certainly the one that is subject to the most intense and constant study, in an effort to keep track of changes in customer attitudes, preferences and demands.

The market is, at the outset, a given precondition, although it may eventually be influenced by products, services, brands or communications. For example, elements of brand communications such as slogans or symbols can be absorbed into the popular consciousness. An understanding of the market conditions and their influence is a necessary prerequisite to any brand development process.

For any notion of differentiation, knowledge of the competition is a basic element. And, using the principles of the holistic approach, six-dimensional knowledge about competitors forms the most complete picture possible. This can reveal not only a competitor's actual position and performance, but the ways in which those targets are achieved. So even if the competitor's positioning has not been achieved by a holistic approach, the effects of all conditions and activities contributing to it can be laid bare by analysis through the six dimensions. This pinpoints areas that can be targeted to obtain competitive advantage.

Market conditions are often the trigger for brand development, which means that this dimension will then be the dominant one in the process. In fact, the marketing function within an organization often has sole responsibility for brand development, and therefore naturally takes the lead. Application of the holistic approach to branding introduces the other dimensions and ensures that a balance is maintained. This also has an effect on definition of the need for market research, which is, on occasion, so voluminous and ill-focused that its practical relevance is not immediately apparent. The holistic branding process allows precise identification of major issues that, although originating in one dimension, have repercussions in others. This fuller knowledge of causes and effects means that specific research, including market research, can be more accurately designed and applied. This implies greater cost-effectiveness as well as clearer and more practically relevant results.

Marketing strategies may need to be revised or renewed as a result of holistic brand development. Achievement of a radical repositioning, for example, will not normally be possible without market communications which promote the brand promise accordingly.

Routes to market are also an important consideration, because transactions occur at most stages along the routes, which can be influential in the brand or identity experience. Whether these are person to person, online, correspondence-based, one-way or two-way, they each present an opportunity to align all experiences with brand values.

Knowledge of the customer base is ever more detailed, and customer relationship management (CRM) has become a vital discipline within brand management. Effective CRM depends on maintaining all dimensions of holistic branding, especially taking into account the prevalence of whole-life product or service offers, one-stop shop approaches, and the vital service back-up to product purchases. Quality monitors, such as the JD Power automobile surveys, demonstrate the impressions made on customer perceptions by the totality of their experiences of a brand.

The internal market, and the concept of the internal customer, are also included within this dimension. Clearly this is related to the cultural and behavioural aspects, but it is worthy of the independent assessment and consideration of its causes and effects.

Design

The word 'design' has, in some cultures, acquired associations of superficiality. This is understandable, particularly in the light of 'designer' labels, and the closely-related concept of 'style'. However, as a dimension of brands and identity, design has a very broad and basic role to perform,

Design

Substance
Design management
Design elements
Processes
Resources
Guidelines

Expression
Characterful
Stylish
Coherent
Ordered
Striking

from the first impact to the lasting, memorable visual impression.

Design formed the root of corporate identification, and the history of visual symbols is the history of civilization. From ancient Egyptian marks through the Christian cross and national flags to corporate logotypes, visual devices have been designed to act as optical triggers to conjure up identification and motivation. They have stirred up strong emotions, both positive and negative, acted as rallying points in time of war, and influenced purchasing decisions in high street shops.

Design in brands and identity is not just to do with symbols and logotypes. A coherent style and consistency creates recognizability and memorability, which are among the primary aims of brand or identity management. Design is the means of obtaining visual consistency, with design management being a vital corporate discipline in achieving this. The complexities of design management often come from the need to balance consistency with flexibility, in order to be able to, say, address different target audiences within the overall corporate or brand design framework. Brand and identity design must also be implemented sensitively and cost-effectively across a wide range of different applications (for example stationery, online media, printed publicity, vehicles, factory signs, and packaging) so that distinctiveness is maintained in spite of the different purposes and physical constraints.

Design must also play its part in differentiation. In an increasingly overcrowded and competitive visual environment, looking different from others is becoming more and more difficult. Registration of new trademarks is now a time-consuming, expensive (in legal costs) and fraught process. Yet still designers manage to come up with original solutions that stand out from the crowd.

Unfortunately, they often do so at the expense of other essential qualities, particularly practical necessities and long-term survival. Practical necessities may be boring, but logotypes and symbols are still appearing which are not reproducible at small sizes, through the fax machine or on the website. And the long-term survival of many is compromised by too strong an influence from the fashions of the day, leading to premature dating and obsolescence.

Fashion and style are obvious elements in design. Clearly, design (and a brand or identity in total) must respond to fashion as part of the visual context as a whole. But, if the recognizability of a brand or identity is to be maintained or strengthened, then there must be a core of continuity to act as the visual trigger. Viewed from the opposite end, there must be the opportunity to adapt to fashions in order to appeal to the tastes and emotions of constantly-changing target audiences. This applies more to fast-moving consumer goods brands than to business-to-business.

This tension between long-term and short-term needs is one of the most dynamic and discussed areas in branding. There are many examples of successes and failures caused by changing or not changing basic design elements, and each must be judged on its merit. But all the indications are that the most successful brands have basic design elements –

| 1900 | 1904 | 1909 | 1930 | 1948 |

| 1955 | 1961 | 1971 | 1995 | 1999 |

Shell's 'pecten' is one of the best-known brand marks in the world.
Its form has been subtly modified over the decades, but it has never lost its recognizability

such as logotypes, symbols and colours – which have lasted for decades. Of course, many have been developed subtly to respond to changes in taste or context, but their core identification features have remained intact.

When real change does occur in an organization, then design reveals another of its uses: it is a powerful signifier of that change. The impact of a new brand or corporate design is always significant, with the first impression often being the most important. Seeing a new letterhead on your desk, or a new sign above your office entrance, is a strong indication that something new is expected inside your organization. Seeing a new pack in the shops, or a new aircraft livery, is an equally potent message of change to the outside world.

In fact, design is a potent ally. It can unite, motivate, signal change or continuity, appeal to the emotions, trigger associations, bring order, differentiate, and sell. However, and this is the crunch, it can only do these things effectively when it is treated strategically and within the context of a holistic brand strategy. As soon as it is seen as separate from the other dimensions, it becomes a superficiality, a magic potion which can somehow be added to make things go better. By the same token, it then becomes dispensable at difficult times.

Creativity (a word that is, wrongly, often treated as synonymous with design) must be applied rationally. Creative decisions must be justifiable in a business context. This is not to rule out innovation, a quality that is essential to progress. But it means that designs should be demonstrably contributing towards strategic goals, and, at a base level, be practical and usable.

Design appeals to what many would say is our primary sense, and certainly the one that frequently gives the first impression. Holistic branding provides the context and strategic basis for design to contribute its full potential.

Communications

In the sense that everything communicates – which is one of the basic propositions of holistic branding – this could be a very broad dimension indeed. However, under this heading we really mean the formal communications, both internal and external, that an organization carries out or commissions. The classical areas are, internally, house magazines, motivational campaigns, the chairperson's speeches, brand-to-life exercises and so on. Externally, the areas include advertising, PR, below-the-line promotions and direct mail. The internal aspects tend to be divided in responsibility between human resources and marketing. The external aspects are typically dealt with by marketing and perhaps corporate affairs, the latter also being responsible for financial and environmental communications, including the relevant annual reports.

Communications

Substance
Internal/external strategies
Media
Messages and content
Target audiences
Plans and budgets

Expression
Relevant
Topical
Credible
Persuasive
Powerful

There is thus much fragmentation within the dimension itself, which a holistic approach can help to identify and focus. The claims of specialists in integrated communications are heard in this area, of course, but there is still the suspicion that this trend is for the convenience and benefit of one-stop shop agencies and networks. In any case, although the integration of formal communications is a worthwhile aim, it is only part of the holistic brand development process.

Examples of fragmentation in communications are rife. Advertising agencies especially are notorious for breaking even simple corporate guidelines for the sake of individual creativity. To some extent, this reflects the short-term/long-term tensions that lie at the heart of sales and marketing activities, and that themselves reflect the day-to-day corporate demands of budget pressures. And this is perhaps why, in a dimension so rich in professional input, there is so much blinkered activity, seeking quick wins, fast bucks, immediate returns from isolated initiatives. In large organizations this creates situations of high internal stress, as brand or marketing managers pursue their own agendas for individual success.

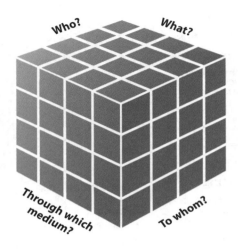

A communications matrix

Externally, it creates confusion and brand weakness.

Internally, similar 'silo thinking' is encountered. Training schemes, for example, often only address specific areas of concern without taking account of the wider picture. Internal communications are frequently the preserve of corporate communications, without reference to, say, the marketing department.

Advertising, PR and all the other ways and means represent significant costs. Singly, they can certainly be effective and lead to increased sales. However, if they do not contribute to the building of a complete picture, long-term, then not only is a potentially valuable synergy lost, but they can actually damage a brand's long-term prospects. At the least, they can blur the image. At worst, they can create cynicism and other negative attitudes, by encouraging false expectations. Viewed from an inclusive angle, communications become one (albeit key) dimension in the whole brand or identity universe.

The process of realizing a holistic brand

There are five basic steps in the holistic branding process:

1. Research and analysis of the status quo and strengths and weaknesses, according to the holistic model
2. Target holistic positioning
3. Gap analysis according to the holistic model, with identification of main action areas
4. Formulation of initiatives
5. Guidelines and standards

The five steps to holistic branding

Step 1	Step 2	Step 3	Step 4	Step 5
Research and analysis	**Target holistic positioning**	**Gap analysis**	**Formulation of initiatives**	**Guidelines and standards**

• Start point statement
• 6-dimensional status quo analysis, including
  – Cultural audit
  – Analysis of existing behaviour and standards
  – Product and/or service review
  – Market research
  – Design audit
  – Communications audit
	• Target brand concept
	• Vision, mission and values
	• Identification of differentiating factors with substance and expression
	• Definition of brand relevance, customer benefits and proposition
	• Market segmentation
		• Gap profile identification between status quo and target
		• Identification and evaluation of discrepancies
		• Establishing of main action areas
			• Culture development
			• Training
			• Brand architecture
			• Brand design
			• Internal and external communications
			• Brand monitoring
			• Product development
			• Market initiatives
			• Etc.
				• Brand management roles and responsibilities
				• Brand portfolio system
				• Communications guidelines
				• Brand design guidelines
				• Brand implementation guidelines
				• Brand performance indicators

At the beginning

Every project begins with an articulation of a problem, a challenge or an opportunity. It might not be stated in succinct terms in writing, and it can manifest itself in any part of the business and its activities. It might be in the figures, in the sales performance, in the perceived image or in staff attitudes. In other words, it might be present in one or more of the six dimensions. Wherever it is, early, broad analysis of the situation via the six dimensions can help to pinpoint it, define the possible scope, and create an outline understanding of the scale and shape of the task necessary to tackle it.

How things stand – holistically

In defining the status quo, and in ordering the information according to the dimensions, we bring the individual areas of concern into sharp relief. This process also reveals their causes and their effects, and equally importantly, the interrelationships between them become clearer. The distinction between substance and expression makes clear any discrepancies or imbalances between reality and conveyed information or characteristics. This is a process of definition and discovery, which results in old assumptions being either confirmed or denied, and in new revelations about the sources of both strengths and weaknesses.

The methods of obtaining information, as opposed to how it is structured, can include secondary, or desk, research, market research, employee research, focus groups and online research. However, for identifying deep-seated issues and encouraging a sense of involvement and acceptance of a project, great stress is placed on management interviews. Carefully planned and sensitively carried out, these not only reveal vital views and attitudes; they can also create positive feelings towards implementation of whatever actions are eventually planned, and act as a catalyst for cultural change.

It is normal to separate internal and external research, but the holistic approach ensures that the two are always considered as sides of a single coin, linked and inseparable. However, internal matters are dealt with first, which is in any case the direction in which brand recognition flows – from the inside to the outside.

Gradually, a complete picture is built up and a high degree of clarity is achieved. The findings may not, of course, be comfortable for everyone, but they will form a true and holistic basis from which to move forward.

How things should be

The holistic approach can be seen as providing a very sophisticated, multi-dimensional 'gap analysis' between what exists and what is desired, in other words between status quo and vision. Because the 'status quo' picture is so complete, the 'vision' picture can be similarly detailed.

Vision	We aim to be Europe's leading personal financial services provider		
Mission	We will achieve this through value-adding, innovative products, focused on customer needs, and delivered consistently		
Values	Responsive, reliable, future-orientated, trustworthy		
	Substance	**Differentiation factors**	Expression
	Global research Worldwide connections Employee potential Technical facilities Off-shore locations	**Resources**	Safe Large Future-orientated International Team-based
	Specific knowledge of financial markets Product knowledge International market intelligence Quality of consultation Cross-selling partners	**Competence**	Professional Qualified Focused Creative Dynamic
	Product portfolio management Assured return on investment Prices Innovations Ability to learn	**Solutions orientated**	Individual Modern Active Efficient Systematic
	Customer orientation Personal advice Customer relationships Initiatives Accessibility	**Service**	Personal Classy Proactive Flexible Inclusive
	Discreetness Fairness Reliability Continuity Partnership	**Trust**	Solid Credible Trustworthy Easy to identify with Rigorous
Customer benefits	Know-how, meeting investment objectives, price-performance ratio, relevance, reassurance and security		
Proposition	Innovators in personal finance, focused on reliable solutions		

The strategic thinking involved in creating the aspirational positioning can be based on full knowledge of all relevant causes and effects. The structure is exactly the same as for the status quo, but the content is updated in line with aspirations and their consequences in all of the six dimensions.

The creation of the strategic and leadership elements, principally the vision, mission and values, is normally the responsibility of top management, supported or facilitated by the involvement of consultants. Interpretation into the day-to-day is carried out in consultation with those closest to such activities, where they will be able to 'own' their initiatives.

The creation of 'operational standards' in all areas affecting day-to-day brand-related activities is the key to implementation of a holistic brand. These standards can be applied to behaviours, management practices, service provision, customer relationship management, performance achievement and so on. They are the assurance that the brand will be thoroughly lived, and that the brand promise will ultimately be delivered to all target audiences.

Holistic brand management

Identification of brand performance indicators, and therefore of initiatives and activities, is only fully possible with reference to results. Holistic brand management therefore introduces two further factors, which work in conjunction with substance and expression: 'experience' and 'achievement'. 'Experience' deals with the perceptions of a brand by various target audiences, both internal and external. 'Achievement' is literally concerned with the achievement of targets, such as market share, price premiums, customer loyalty and sales.

When the four factors are combined as a cycle, and evaluated in relation to the six dimensions, individually and as a whole, then it becomes possible to pinpoint key brand performance indicators. Measures can be introduced where necessary, and then be monitored on an ongoing basis to provide proof of success, or otherwise.

There is a clear top-management responsibility to keep the overall goal in view, and to ensure that measures are continually implemented and meas-

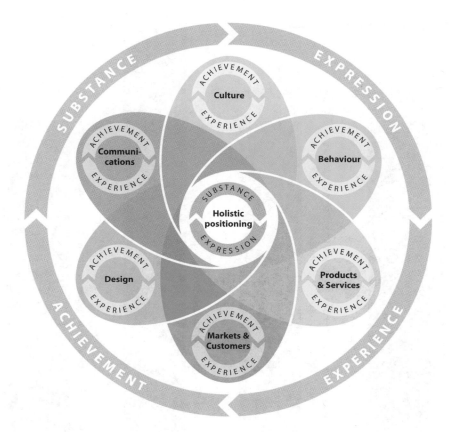

Through the holistic approach, brand performance indicators can
be identified within each dimension, then applied as a whole

ured according to key brand performance indicators that support the holistic positioning. If this is done, there will be wide-ranging benefits throughout the organization, resulting in every appropriate resource making its
individual contribution towards the target brand.

Guided by process management tools for specific problem situations,
the task is made transparent and facilitated, although it is inevitably an
intensive and in-depth activity, and therefore demands a high degree of
commitment from the organization itself.

Process management tools

Culturescan is applied to the analysis, definition, development and management of brand and corporate cultures.

Evaluation	Definition	Development of strategy	Culture deployment	Monitoring
Visions, targets, strategies	Market imperatives	Vision, mission & values	Change management	Assessment
Values & standards	Organisational demands	Targets	Workshops	Feedback measures
Buy-in/conflict potential	Structures & processes	Indicators	Project support	Reinforcement

Corporatefocus is applied to the development of a holistic positioning as the basis for leadership and staff motivation, for differentiation from competitors, and for the development of brand and corporate identities.

Analysis	Positioning	Measures	Implementation	Monitoring
Market & competitors	Vision, mission & values	Leadership & behaviour	Change management	Assessment
Staff attitudes	Differentiation factors	Communications	Workshops	Feedback measures
Existing position	Substance & expression	Brand expression	Coaching	Reinforcement
	Customer benefits			
	Proposition			

Brandadvantage is applied to the strategic development of corporate, product, or service brands.

Analysis	Positioning	Naming	Design	Implementation	Portfolio management
Market and competitors	Vision, mission & values	Evaluation	Evaluation	Strategic goal setting	Evaluation
Products & services	Differentiation factors	New name creation	Development	Processes	Strategy
Culture and behaviour	Substance & expression		Renewal	Responsibilities	Monitoring & development
	Customer benefits				
	Proposition				

Identitystructure is applied to the strategic management of complex structures and portfolios of brands, names or identities.

Evaluation	Definition	Positioning	Concepts	Implementation
Existing structures	Target groups	Vision, mission & values	Structures	Guidelines
Names & brands	Segments	Differentiation factors	Verbal or visual elements	Communications
Goals	Hierarchies	Substance & expression	Strategic management	Monitoring & feedback
		Customer benefits		
		Proposition		

Communications**key** is applied to the development of comprehensive communications management strategies for brands and companies: who says what, to whom, through which media.

Evaluation
Strategies
Messages & media
Structures

Definition
Positioning
Segmentation of audiences
Internal factors

Development
Content
Communications matrix
Style

Strategy
Measures
Media
Implementation plan

Implementation
Strategy
Guidelines
Monitoring

Customer**first** is applied to the development of customer focus, customer relationship management (CRM), and customer service or quality standards to improve customer satisfaction.

Evaluation
Industry standards
Competitors
Status quo

Definition
Positioning
Customer profiles
Relevant quality aspects

Development
Activity areas
Delivery characteristics
Structures & processes

Formulation
Standards
Measures
Control

Implementation
Action plan
Communication
Feedback & monitoring

Holistic**Brandmanager** is applied to the ongoing management of a brand, enabling individual and collective analysis and monitoring of the six dimensions from four relevant perspectives, including identification of, and measurement by, Brand Performance Indicators (BPIs).

Analysis
Market & competitors
Existing position
Industry standards

Positioning
Vision, mission & values
Differentiation factors
Substance & expression
Customer benefits
Proposition

Perspectives
Substance
Expression
Experience
Achievement

BPIs
Quality & efficiency
Appropriateness & consistency
Relevance & satisfaction
Growth & profitability

Measures
Conceptualise
Construct & test
Implement

Monitoring
Measurement
Evaluation
Action

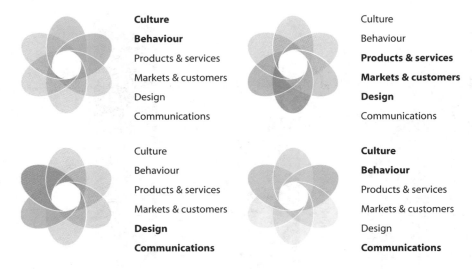

Culture	Culture
Behaviour	Behaviour
Products & services	**Products & services**
Markets & customers	**Markets & customers**
Design	**Design**
Communications	Communications

Culture	**Culture**
Behaviour	**Behaviour**
Products & services	Products & services
Markets & customers	Markets & customers
Design	Design
Communications	**Communications**

In practice, attention will mostly be focused on one or several of the dimensions, depending on the individual situation

Balancing the dimensions

Although the dimensions have so far been listed with equal emphasis, different situations demand unequal consideration. For example, the cultural factors or service delivery may be the problem areas in one case, whereas in another the communications or design aspects may be the major cause of concern. This will naturally bias the structure and content of any project towards the relevant areas, but consideration according to the six dimensions, even if only as documentation of the status quo, will put all one, two, three, four or five-dimensional problems into a full, holistic context.

It is also the case that when the starting point, or the most obvious problem or opportunity, is present in one dimension only, contributory factors or further opportunities may be found in other dimensions. This is an example of the optimization potential of holistic branding, of its synergy-creating action. Even at such an early stage in the process, it helps to prevent those destructive mismatches that regularly occur, for instance, between the brand promise and individual behaviour.

A decade of success

In the decade since the holistic approach was devised, we have put it into practice in numerous situations, and it has always brought benefits: some expected, others unexpected. Particular challenges that have been met include the following:

- A global chemical and pharmaceuticals company of 45,000 employees whose culture did not support its new corporate communications strategy.
- An international infrastructure consultancy whose culture was not appropriate to new market circumstances and which suffered from a fragmented identity caused by repeated acquisitions.
- A European bank seeking to reposition its private banking offer to take advantage of new market opportunities.
- A charitable hospital foundation with a need to balance, within its identity, religious and secular values and goals.
- A forced merger between two former competing raw materials suppliers, leading to a need for a new unifying vision, a changed culture and a new multi-brand strategy.

The striking thing about these examples, superficially, is their differences. Indeed, each situation is wholly different, as each organization is different. Just as in medicine each patient must be considered as an individual, so in considering its brand, each organization is unique. Any process must be almost infinitely flexible to be relevant and beneficial in all these varied circumstances.

However, all the examples mentioned here involved consideration of the six dimensions of holistic branding. They were progressed according to the same broad principles and, in some parts of the process, even using similar tools, although these were individualized for each and every circumstance. In each example, the structure imposed by the six dimensions gave an entirely new and different perspective of completeness and of interrelationships.

Holistic branding is a proven success in many and various situations, providing a whole range of benefits. A 'holistic positioning' is quite different from a

conventional market positioning and provides an aspirational blueprint across all six dimensions, making the vital link between the brand vision and the practical means of delivering it. Leadership and implementation are embraced within the holistic brand management process to gain the support of all in enabling every possible resource to make its individual contribution towards the target positioning, and to delivering the brand promise.

Chapter 3
Pressing Issues, Inclusive Solutions

Relevance and urgency

Some of the global brand issues which have arisen in recent years could have been predicted, others not. Some issues, such as the quantification of brand value, are deep-rooted, and remain to challenge us. Some developed gradually; others took us by surprise, for example the speed of the development of the Internet. Generally, the pace of change and the intensity of competition has lent a new urgency to facing all of them.

There are issues, for example the management of change, that can be numbered among the great business issues of the age. There are others, such as the online and offline debate, which may only occupy us until we are more comfortable in accommodating new technologies as part of an everyday communications spectrum. But in all of the issues we have encountered, the adoption of a holistic viewpoint opens up new perspectives which bring problems, and their solutions, into focus.

This is in no way to suggest that the approach is an easy 'cure all' because, as we have seen, the complexity of applying its processes is considerable and the exact content varies from case to case. But in many cases the benefits achieved were exactly those that were desired at the outset, and in some they were much greater and more diverse than had been envisaged.

We have observed that, in relation to present and known future challenges, the holistic approach provides a framework, a navigation chart, even a checklist, which supports the optimization of management and business processes through its influence on attitudes and its strategic deployment of corporate resources. In other words, it is a cost-effective, proven way of setting goals, aligning attitudes, delivering the brand promise and communicating the benefits. In the next pages, we raise some brand and identity-related challenges and issues, all of which are current and pressing. In each case, the holistic approach is an appropriate and relevant way to view, and then to deal with, the problems and opportunities.

The challenge of the global brand

Is the idea of a global brand worth pursuing? Can globalizing a brand save money, or make money, or is it a high risk strategy with a significant downside? Many companies have little choice. Small home markets, restricted market segments or the economics of large-scale production mean that international expansion is an inevitable growth strategy.

Global brands with national associations

There are few truly global brands, of course, perhaps because there are even fewer companies that are not linked in the mind with one country or another. There are brands with a national association that are sold worldwide – consumer brands such as Nike or automobile brands such as Mercedes-Benz – but they are often viewed differently in different markets.

Nevertheless, all brands sold internationally must address cultural issues relating to internal and external target groups in order to succeed in widely differing environments and, at the same time, retain some common core values. Coordinated consideration of the six dimensions of the holistic approach provides the essential basis for dealing with this multi-cultural minefield. The process also provides an involving way to encourage overseas subsidiaries or partners to develop their own interpretations of visions or brand values, for application in their own circumstances, at the same time as the control mechanisms to deliver the same brand promise everywhere. Developed in this way, brand values are more likely to be adopted locally than through edicts from distant head offices, and the risks of errors of cultural judgement are much reduced.

Very often, much more common ground is established than was originally thought possible, and an atmosphere of constructive collaboration is created. In this atmosphere, the potential of a global brand is much more likely to be achieved and, sometimes just as important, the pitfalls are more likely to be avoided.

The big issue: costs

The cost issue is never irrelevant. In good times it is important and in bad times it is an inescapable hurdle, and is often used as the excuse for cutting spending on promotion or brand development. If this happens, then there is the usual bleating about maintaining spending in a recession to prepare for the eventual recovery. There may also be presentation of evidence to support the argument to spend on brands in a downturn. But if this is done only one-sidedly, not on the basis of a holistic strategy, it will fall on deaf ears.

The one-sidedness stems from the fact that the spending under consideration is usually that of the marketing department, which will include advertising, direct mail, design, promotional print and other externally-biased brand-building activities. The spending is clearly identifiable, apparent and therefore straightforward to reduce or cut. Not only will the financial director be satisfied, but the shareholders will see that action has been taken to reduce costs in a very visible way. In the short term, the savings are clear, and whatever is said in an attempt to uphold promotional spending in a recession, the evidence shows that advertising agencies, design groups and the like suffer at these times.

Holistic branding is, at the same time, more effective and less obvious. Because the whole effort is not solely focused on classical communications, and because the concept, means and measures are knitted into the day-to-day activities, they are not so readily identified as add-on elements and are therefore not so subject to summary cuts. Even if certain aspects are reduced or eliminated, the effect on the whole is unlikely to be so severe. But the real cost benefit of the holistic approach comes from the fact that it presses into use all the resources that can possibly be used to build a brand or identity. For less cost, the effect can be the same. For the same cost, the effect can be greater.

It is this efficient use – or optimization – of resources that sets the holistic approach apart. It is like the atoms in a magnet: all pointing in the same direction to attract the target. It is efficient because, in the end, everything a company does can be in support of the brand, or not. Either way, it costs the same, but the result is very different. Diffusion of the brand destroys value; consistency creates it.

Transparency

Real or imagined, transparency has become a goal and a requirement: transparency of corporate structures, of processes, of dealings, of interests. Flatter corporate structures have reduced hierarchies and shortened lines of command. Individual responsibility for defined areas of action has replaced the carrying out of orders. Individual target groups, such as shareholders or employees, overlap or merge to create the much broader concept of a 'stakeholder'. In this dynamic and democratic environment, it becomes hugely more challenging to influence attitudes and behaviour while, ironically, the need for shared attitudes and brand-led behaviour has never been greater.

Because the holistic branding process is essentially inclusive, it offers a way to take advantage of a culture of transparency, as well as contribute towards it. Creation of visions, establishment of corporate or brand values, interpretation of brand values into individual working practices, devising standards of customer services or behaviour: all these can be transparent elements within a holistic brand management strategy.

The concepts of 'internal branding' or 'living the brand' are often only training or communications-led approaches to the alignment of behaviour and performance with brand values. These are consequently largely superficial, dealing with external manifestations rather than internal drivers. Holistic branding, with its inclusive view and involving processes, replaces such opaque, compartmentalized approaches with a high degree of transparency, perfectly attuned to the corporate environment of the twenty-first century. The approach is also therefore compatible with flatter corporate structures, where cause and effect are more subtle than in old-style hierarchies.

The brand-led company

If the brand is the key to success, then the brand-led company is the corollary. The brand may, of course, be that of the company itself or of one of its products or services, but the requirement is the same: the company must be led and managed in order to increase the value of the brand or brands, and therefore of the company itself.

Effective management demands information and tools: the holistic approach supplies both, in full. The status quo can be scrutinized in all of the six dimensions, and to reveal the effects between them. For example, the likely effect of an existing culture on a proposed corporate strategy can be assessed. Expressions of the culture in various areas of the business, and externally, can be evaluated, pinpointing areas of strength and weakness. Similarly, the internal and external effects of corporate behaviour can be mapped and understood, as can the effects of external communications. From all of this information a strategic direction can be conceptualized, which is in turn put into action through specific means and measures, again within the six dimensions.

The dimensions themselves, and the initiatives and operational standards within them, provide an action plan. The vision and values give the strategic intent and the 'attitude template', for reaching goals and targets. The whole is a sophisticated brand identity management system that supports the role of the corporate leadership. This is not to be seen in any way as a kind of manipulative method of influencing attitudes and behaviour, but as a sound interpretation of leadership principles, and the encouragement of identification with, and shared acceptance of, a vision. It is as much about empowerment and a coordinated search for goals and meaningful cooperation, as it is about communications and external image-building.

The comprehensiveness of the holistic approach demands leadership responsibility, but then facilitates strategies and action.

Online or off?

This may be a more transient issue than some others, but online brands have become a matter of high concern. In the white heat of technological advance, however, certain basic facts have been banished from the general consciousness.

The first fact is that the fundamental laws of communication and identification apply online, just as they do to every channel ever invented. For instance, you must be able to access information when you need it; you must be able to see, hear or read, and understand, what is presented; you must be able to recognize or identify the source of the material; and so on. We can all attest to the fact that early 'webmasters' did not have these rules front of mind when they created many of the multi-layered, impenetrable and fashion-led websites that we have all struggled with, or given up on.

The second is that all of the communications channels available to a brand must be considered as a whole in order to achieve the desired strength of profile and accuracy of positioning. This applies even if the online channel itself is addressed to different target segments from those at whom offline communications are directed. These segments are not watertight and much overlap will occur, both at any given time and over a period of time.

However, if these basic points are met, there is still the issue of branding of online 'products' or services. These can be divided into online services from existing providers, for example banks, and newly-created online providers, such as Amazon.com, lastminute.com and many others. Banks are a good example of the opportunities and pitfalls. People trust online banks significantly less than their bricks-and-mortar equivalents. We surmise that this is because trust and security are the prime qualities that bank customers require, and that the web – partly because of a series of highly publicized incidents – is not seen as a secure environment, and therefore is not to be trusted. The extrapolated consequence of this for branding is that it would be more reassuring for customers if a bank's online channel were branded as its own, rather than as a newcomer. And, indeed, the multi-channel bank has become an accepted model, although not a universal one.

The 'trust' aspect also means that newcomers to the web must work that much harder to establish their brands in order to compensate for the perceived weakness in this quality. We can see this in the fact that the take-up for most online offers has been less enthusiastic than predicted. It is one thing to surf, it is another to enter your credit card details and press the 'order' button.

Bricks and clicks

A study commissioned by Henrion Ludlow Schmidt from ICM in July 2000 showed that only 7 per cent of people trusted online banks. We concluded that the findings had far-reaching implications for those responsible for creating lasting and credible online brands.

Question: Which do you trust most, the older high-street bank brands or the new online ones?

	Total %	Age 18–24 %	Age 55–64 %	Interested users %
Older high-street bank brands	73	75	82	58
New online ones	7	15	5	15
Neither	14	8	10	23
Don't know	5	2	2	4

The online branding of a multi-channel bank, or the online branding of an organization in any other business area, brings with it the inter-dependence and interactivity of all dimensions. The culture and behaviour of an organization are not absent or undetectable in a website, and what use is a superb online presentation if the fulfilment is disappointing? The fact is that an online presence must express a brand's values in all possible ways, including ease of use, portrayal of subjective qualities, use of language and consistency with all other media.

Online aspects would, of course, be included in any consideration of 'integrated communications'. But, as we said in the first chapter, integrated communications are only part of the story, and holistic branding is so much more. We would claim that online activities can only achieve their full potential through application of, and as part of, a holistic brand strategy.

Managing change

Brand management, as often as not, is part of change management, especially when it concerns the corporate brand. Mergers, acquisitions, IPOs, MBOs and restructurings all involve branding as a major element, along with all of the other strategic, financial and operational concerns. Unfortunately (again), branding is often treated as the icing on the cake, the final piece of decoration which completes the picture. The holistic branding process, in contrast, can be a catalyst in the whole scenario, dealing with the soft issues and promoting the vital changes in attitudes and culture that are the prerequisite for success.

In merger situations, for example (and therefore in acquisitions, which most 'mergers' actually are), it is well accepted that the failure of cultures to adapt and meld is one of the main causes of difficulty, and it is cited as one of the major culprits causing some to fail. It seems that, while the hard factors such as economies of scale, staff numbers and profit forecasts are readily quantified and dealt with, soft factors like culture present major problems.

It is not that the culture problem is unrecognized. It is just that the ways of measuring and influencing it have been, on the one hand, notoriously imprecise and flabby and, on the other hand, often the preserve of the human resources department. With a bias towards one dimension, this inevitably produces a one-sided view of the situation which is generally not consciously aligned with external brand values.

Holistic branding sees culture as one dimension of a complete approach. It takes account of the fact that other dimensions, such as market conditions and strategies, will have an effect on the culture and will be affected by the culture. And the process, being involving and transparent, exposes all such influences and then supplies the means to shape them. Even if the recommended activities are in only one or two of the dimensions, full awareness of the causes and effects in other dimensions will lead to a more effective response. For example, in a merger situation, it may be necessary to deal with any or all of the following:

- attitudes of resentment and resistance
- cultural mismatch, leading to lack of cooperation
- inflexible attitudes preventing realization of merger potential
- loss of competition target (the other merger partner), resulting in the need for new targets and a new vision
- major brands of a combined operation need strategic decisions about the future: should they be combined or kept separate?
- strategic decisions on name and identity: to retain, combine or renew.

Whereas these can be viewed as separate problems, they are all part of the same picture and are interdependent. Providing a new vision and target, for example, will assist in bringing cultures together. Solving the name issues will enable everyone to march under the same flag. And the holistic process applied in doing this will, in itself, encourage cooperation and collaboration.

Change is unavoidable but always risky, by its nature. The holistic approach offers a way to minimize such risk, and maximize the realization of potential. It does this through the comprehensiveness of the dimensions and the involving nature of the process, ensuring that change is a managed phenomenon, aligned with corporate and brand values.

The vision thing

We all need a vision. We cannot work without purpose. If we try, then we go round in circles, we repeat ourselves or we just cannot get started. In business terms that is plain wasteful, inefficient, costly – and destructive of motivation, focus and value. A shared intent is essential in order to progress towards a goal.

However, it has to be admitted that corporate statements about visions have not been viewed with the greatest admiration in all quarters. Visions are, of course, nearly always associated with values, and then grouped accordingly. Much debate has centred around the semantics of these words, along with the word 'mission', and our own definition is given in the context of the holistic approach.

So what is it that has created such apathy – even animosity – in some quarters towards these expressions of good intent? A principal objection is that good intent is often all that they represent, with very little relevance to what the organization really does or, more particularly, to what employees do from day to day or to how they experience the organization. This perceived irrelevance can be traced to four causes:

- **Generalization:** the statements could apply to any organization. They are often dismissed as 'motherhood' statements, lists of universal goodnesses that do not differentiate, captivate or motivate. They can only be seen as the cynical meanderings of a disconnected management.
- **Lack of realism:** the aspirations are too far removed from reality to be achieved without some kind of corporate revolution, date unspecified. The result is at best statements that have no credibility, and at worst statements that are treated as a joke.
- **Irrelevance:** no connection is made between the statement and day-to-day activities. The result is a 'so what?' reaction, the statement being largely ignored and forgotten.
- **Not invented here:** if employees or even managers have had no hand in creating the statements, or have not been witness to a transparent process, then they are unlikely to adopt the results wholeheartedly.

The holistic approach is to incorporate the vision, as well as the mission and values, into the holistic positioning, as described in Chapter 2. This gives the vision a central role as the driving force and direction-giver, while the values are made to work hard as the basis for brand substance and expression, as well as acting as the basis for all sorts of strategic decisions and measures. There is a direct follow-through from the vision to the operational standards, via the values. Consistency thus leads to credibility. In this way, the foundation is laid for delivery of the brand promise, for focused and positive brand perceptions – and on to added brand value.

A final word on vision from the seminal book *Built to Last* by James Collins and Jerry Porras: 'The essence of a visionary company comes in the translation of its core ideology and its own unique drive for progress into the very fabric of the organization – into goals, strategies, tactics, policies, processes, cultural practises, management behaviors, building layouts, pay systems, accounting systems, job design – into everything that the company does.' That is a good description of holistic branding.

Brand value

That brands are important and provide benefits is hardly ever at issue. The specific value of brands, or of an individual brand, often is. How do you measure the value of a brand? It is of course a very obvious and fair question, but there is no simple answer. Value is, after all, always relative. There is, however, one myth that should be disposed of straight away: that there is a reliable formula to measure the financial, or balance sheet, value of a brand.

The need to place a financial value on a brand is clear, in terms of evaluating such an asset at the time of, say, a takeover bid. Nestlé's assessment of the worth of Rowntrees, the York-based chocolate company, was heavily biased by the value of the Kit-Kat brand. Indeed, brand value was probably the main reason for the purchase. Calculations and negotiations are inevitable in such cases, but problems can occur when companies seek to put brand valuations on their balance sheets, for the purpose of influencing their market capitalizations. This is not an accounting discussion, but it is striking how different valuation methods come up with very different figures (see page 2). In the end, raw financial value can only be ascertained according to the prevailing conditions at the time of any deal, together with negotiations involving bankers and lawyers.

The most relevant, and most strategically valuable, measurement must be based on meaningfully identified brand value drivers in all dimensions. If one is really to know and understand the value – in the broadest and most relevant terms – of a brand, then one-dimensional measurement will not suffice. The prerequisite to a meaningful measurement is to know the real drivers of brand value, which can be identified by analysis of causes and effects within the six dimensions of holistic branding. These drivers, which we call 'Brand Performance Indicators' (BPIs), once established, can be tracked over a period of time, thus forming a multi-dimensional, dynamic measurement of a brand's true performance, and therefore value.

There is no instance where the holistic approach is irrelevant, and no issue where application of its principles will not provide advantages over more limited views of branding. Holistic branding responds to all challenges, helping to clarify the analysis of complex situations as well as providing a concept and implementation framework that is broad and comprehensive enough to face any issue. Holistic branding is the only approach that recognizes fully that branding is a strategic management tool of the first rank.

Chapter 4
In Real Life

The cases that follow bring concepts to life – or life to concepts. They are not necessarily all conceived according to the structure or methods of the holistic approach, but they do show that the idea of inclusive branding has inevitably found its way into all sorts of organizations; that they are already waking up to the interdependences of different dimensions of branding, and seeing at least some of the benefits they can achieve.

As real-life stories, written by people at the heart of brand matters in leading organizations, they reflect the problems, opportunities, ideas and successes that are all part of the challenge of brands. Overwhelmingly, however, there is a sense of a fresh realization and confidence that brands are at the root of success and must therefore be considered at the highest levels and accorded appropriate resources. There is also a sense that brand thinking now permeates corporate strategic activities, and that branding must respond to immediate, and new, challenges and opportunities, helping to exploit them to advantage.

The cases cover a wide variety of industries and business areas. The problem situations are all different and the starting points vary. Those responsible are from different professions or have different job titles, although they all have responsibility for the brands concerned. And the symptoms, as well as the solutions, occurred in different dimensions, both internal and external. But they all have this in common: they demonstrate that the future of branding depends on a realization that everything possible must be made to pull in the same direction, towards the target positioning. Only in this way will brands meet the high expectations placed on them, and only in this way will brand promises be fulfilled.

The cases

When global brands are being discussed, then **Mercedes-Benz** is always held out as a paragon of brand value. With its German origins, and its impeccable engineering heritage, it regularly tops tables of global super-brands. Now a part of DaimlerChrysler, the Mercedes-Benz brand needs to focus on its values, communicate these to all stakeholders, and ensure consistent implementation around the world. See chapter 5, page 60.

Although owned by different parents during its short history, the **Orange** brand has established a strong and distinctive positioning, as well as being outstandingly successful. Entering an ultra-competitive market already dominated by the leading players, Orange created a brand world of its own, concentrating on the creation and expression of an innovative, customer-focused offer. The brand is respected and widely seen as a benchmark. See chapter 6, page 78.

During its long history as a provider of health insurance, **BUPA** became almost a generic in this field in the UK. To take advantage of changes in the market, however, BUPA needed to change long-held perceptions in order to broaden its offer into areas that were not its perceived competence. Thus the company embarked on a major brand repositioning exercise. This encompassed a whole range of holistic meas-ures, from the changing of staff and management attitudes to a new brand hierarchy and an advertising campaign. See chapter 7, page 95.

The sport and leisure industries are poised for tremendous growth. Within sport, there is no stronger brand than **Manchester United**. Of course, to speak of a football club as a brand would have been impossible until relatively recently, but that is how this renowned name is now managed. Expressed through marketing and brand experience, Manches-ter United is portrayed as highly professional, confident and, of course, successful. Results on the pitch will always be to some extent unpre-dictable, but the brand creates loyalty and enthusiasm which transcends the ups and downs of competition. See chapter 8, page 112.

Of all British brands, **Virgin** must be the most discussed and debated. Inseparably linked to its founder, Richard Branson, Virgin has always acted in a way true to its principles, and has never been afraid to proclaim what it stands for, in the most visible manner. To speak of subtlety in relation to Virgin seems incongruous, but the brand has been developed with great sophistication. Several times in its lifespan, disaster has been predicted because of this brand extension or that new project, but the core values – together with clever, creative PR and marketing – have always pulled it through. See chapter 9, page 129.

Another area besides football clubs where to speak of a brand was not usual until recently is law firms. In the comprehensive nature of its approach to the subject, **CMS** must be seen as something of a pioneer. Professional services organizations often have a problem with the concept of differentiation, but CMS went to the root of this by dealing first with its vision, mission and values in a successful attempt to define itself within the market. Every other dimension of branding then followed, all built on a convincing and credible foundation. See chapter 10, page 147.

As a premium brand, **Miele**, the German appliances and kitchens manufacturer, found itself with a reputation which, fortunately, was based on its values, not on specific products. This is therefore largely a story of the careful nurturing of brand values during a period of planned organic growth. However, it also demonstrates that brand extension must be based on inclusive principles to ensure that the brand promise is always met. In this sense, there may be more to lose than to gain in such exercises, and the holistic branding process safeguards what has been built up over many years. See chapter 11, page 164.

Rejuvenation of a brand that was neglected over a long period of time, as well as sharing a brand name with a separate business, is what the **Dunlop Sport** story is all about. Once associated with famous names, particularly in tennis and golf, Dunlop lost direction in the 1980s, in terms of both its product and consequently its link with stars of the day. The interdependence of these aspects, and others, shows again that the reality of inclusive branding is here. Dunlop's 'rejuvenation team' included top management from the marketing, logistics, finance, sales, human resources and manufacturing functions, in a successful attempt to break down barriers and optimize the available – and considerable – resource. See chapter 12, page 182.

Chapter 5
The Best or Nothing: Mercedes-Benz

Hans-Georg Brehm
Head of Brand Management

A car like no other

The present position of Mercedes-Benz as the world's leading premium car brand is practically beyond dispute: within just a few years, unit sales of cars have grown by almost half to more than one million worldwide. Image research studies place the brand at the peak of prestige worldwide; increasingly respected studies of brand value place Mercedes-Benz right at the top among car brands. Once again, customers must wait more than a year for delivery of new products such as the SL. The profits generated by the Mercedes-Benz divisions are a secure source of funds for the whole DaimlerChrysler Group.

Wolfgang Reitzle, a former member of the BMW Board and until recently head of Ford's Premier Automotive Group which contains luxury brands Volvo, Aston Martin, Jaguar, Land Rover, Lincoln and Mercury, writes as follows in his book *Luxury Creates Affluence*: 'Amongst all car brands Mercedes is certainly … the one it would be least easy to damage. This brand can withstand a great deal and … is so valuable precisely because it allows a high volume to be achieved together with high prices.'

Why has the brand with the star achieved such mythical status while remaining commercially successful at the same time?

Number one right from the start

It was certainly not commercial success that marked the beginning of automotive development, but the unbending determination and passion of a few ingenious and stubborn, yet otherwise very different, characters. Personalities like these are a precondition for the success of any company or brand.

Gottlieb Daimler pursued the epoch-making idea of accelerating literally everything – including progress – with his compact, fast-running and mobile engine: cycles, ships, coaches, airships, trams. Carl Benz – and his wife Bertha – were the real car pioneers. Less than 100 kilometres from Daimler's workshop they laboured tirelessly to produce the first operational and roadworthy automobile. Wilhelm Maybach, Daimler's comrade-in-arms, was probably the most ingenious designer of his time and Emil Jellinek, the Austrian Consul General and Daimler representative in Nice, was the epitome of the marketing man. Not only did he drive Maybach to produce better and better, more efficient designs which were superior to other vehicles, he also used the popular pastime of motor racing as evidence of their performance and made an automobile brand really famous for the first time by giving it the name of one of his daughters, Mercedes.

He also gave his attention to suitable clientele: well-heeled and ambitious gentleman drivers such as Prince Heinrich, brother of the German Kaiser – who may incidentally be credited with the invention of the windscreen wiper – Franz Josef I of Austria and the Maharaja of Jodhpur. At the wheel of the oldest Mercedes that still exists today, a 1902 Mercedes Simplex, William K. Vanderbilt Jr reached the unbelievable speed of 111.2 km/h. This sort of performance and clientele ensured that the well-heeled knew which car was a must in their social circle.

What a heritage: the first two cars in the world, the first vehicle resembling a motorcycle, the first bus, the first truck, the first taxi, the first Mercedes – a gigantic success. In other words, here was a premium brand from the start, one which was technically superior, famous, popular and expensive all at the same time – a car for the connoisseur.

Highs and lows

Real personalities and real innovations were the driving forces for success. However, there were also those who gained fame but still failed. There have been more than 1,000 car brands, only a few dozen of which still exist today. The basis for this phenomenon is perseverance. Overcoming disappointments and crises, and emerging stronger than before; making fewer mistakes than the competitors; success as a sequence of mastered crises, and also as a long road paved with highlights: racing victories in the early days, in the 1930s and 1950s; famous cars such as the 300 SL or the SSK; safety developments like the passenger cell, ABS or ESP; the development of fuel injection and the diesel engine for cars; the definition of the automotive luxury class by world standards. Without this inventive spirit and persistence in the search for the best possible solution, there would be no Mercedes-Benz, not to mention a whole range of automotive conveniences which we now take for granted. 'Enduring passion' with the German penchant for perfectionism and a willingness to meet the wishes of customers all over the world have become major characteristics.

The birth of the star

Naturally there was no planning of identity features in the early years. However, there was always a search for a certain symbolism that would lend expression to the claim to leadership in technical progress and success. Mercedes has existed as a brand name since 1901. The origin of the star as a trademark is ascribed to Gottlieb Daimler. It was he who first drew a three-pointed star on a postcard to his family, with the comment 'and this star will one day shed its blessing on my achievements'. The three points are taken to symbolize motorization on land, on water and in the air.

Following the merger between the Daimler and Benz companies in 1926, the two names became one, with Daimler-Benz as the company and Mercedes-Benz as the brand. The trademarks were also merged, the Benz laurel wreath and new company name surrounding the star as a ring. To the present day every Mercedes-Benz vehicle bears this historic trademark in addition to the star on the radiator.

The extent to which this trademark has contributed to the success of Mercedes has never really been examined. Naturally, there is no way of separating the two, as performance and symbolism are indissolubly wedded, and continuously strengthen each other. There is an ever-present link: the aesthetic appeal and attraction of the star as a symbol that is understood worldwide without the need for words, and the challenge that a product bearing this star is expected to meet. There is probably no symbol used as a brand which is as elegant, as easily recognizable even in scribbled form, as indestructible and as unmistakable. Accordingly, the star has hardly changed over the decades, and embodies continuity throughout all the company's developments.

There is something else: colour. The story has the quality of a legend but is nonetheless true. In the first Grand Prix of the 1934 racing season, at the Nürburgring, the Mercedes-Benz team was shocked by the realization that its new cars exceeded the weight limit. As a last resort, the white paint was scraped off the cars overnight, white having been the usual colour of German racing cars until that time. The cars lined up at the start next day in the original colour of their light-alloy bodies: silver. One of them won the race and the name 'Silver Arrow' was born. With it came the third identity element that was here to stay: the colour silver.

Lasting success and historically grown identity symbols facilitate identification with the brand character among both the public and the staff. The approach to perfection unites customers, engineers and mechanics; the large, attractive, fast and proud cars boost the status of staff and owners alike. The 'identity' becomes taken for granted and is reflected in everyday activities.

From radiator mascot to today's brand mark: relatively few steps over a whole century

The brand positioning of Mercedes-Benz

The pole position, leadership and superior prestige of Mercedes-Benz became practically unassailable. However, by the early 1990s competitors in Europe and Japan had gained ground with sportiness, elegance, high-tech features, driving pleasure, quality and favourable prices. Mercedes-Benz was being pushed into the pipe-and-slippers segment, with younger buyers and women thin on the ground. The product range in the car sector was limited to conventional saloons, middle-aged coupés and practical estate cars. The future was to be very different!

A new, far-reaching growth strategy was adopted. Complacency made way for customer orientation. New products in a host of new segments were developed and a learning drive supported the introduction of lean design and production methods. None of the competing brands was, or is, able to point to a comparable foundation of values. Quality, safety, comfort, durability – these were strengths that had to be defended and consolidated. They were defined as indispensable and characteristic 'basic values'.

It was clearly recognized that individualization to a high standard would become an even more decisive buying criterion in the future. Mercedes-Benz uses the term 'trend values' to describe this set of values, which are not followed slavishly in the manner of fashion, but are met by means of emotional interior and exterior designs, a wide variety of appointments, different vehicle concepts and a wider range of performance characteristics.

A third, increasingly important, set of values is in the area of social attitudes. Public acceptance of size, performance, speed and energy consumption is increasingly dependent on a willingness to meet society's demands for the conservation of resources, and not only by following government regulations. In this respect Mercedes-Benz defines itself with a number of 'orientation values'. The summarized positioning is as follows:

- Mercedes-Benz is the most desirable brand in the automotive world, unsurpassed in quality, innovation and fascination; authentic in its basic values, exciting in its trend values, visionary in its orientation values – and passionate in attitude.

- This range of values covers the entire structure of the psychologically-identified needs that are relevant for a premium car brand, translates them into automotive benefits and makes them – like many positioning models – interchangeable. So, then, four supplementary aspects make the positioning special:
  a. All these emotional and rational values are combined into an attitude of openness, continuous commitment and fairness which has always characterized the brand and forms the unseen link between the workforce, the company and its products.
  b. The assurance that only Mercedes-Benz with its heritage and capabilities is able to devote itself wholeheartedly to such a comprehensive mission.
  c. The specific weighting of these aspects which only applies for Mercedes-Benz.
  d. The simplified visual representation of this sophisticated and complex value system as a circle with segments which can be used for the brand as a whole, to define individual model series and services and for communication purposes.

Communication to signal a new departure

Developing automobiles takes years, previously six to eight years and still two to four years nowadays. Sheer complexity and the need to ensure reliability in the premium sector limit the scope to accelerate the process. This means that any plan for a significant change requires staying power and strong nerves over a longer time period.

Mercedes-Benz is certain of its approach, and communication can prepare the way for success. Amenable, reticent, confirmatory advertising was replaced by a self-assured brand presence. Advertising budgets were practically doubled, almost reaching the level sustained by competitors for years. The international motor shows in Geneva, Frankfurt, Detroit and Tokyo became showcases for the ability of the brand to look to the future. Motor racing as a worldwide competition between the leaders, and a fun factor for car fans, became a media event which constantly brought new heroes to the fore. Sponsoring and placement in sport, culture and films brought both products and brand into the here and now.

There was an immediate gain in public attention for Mercedes-Benz. Perceptions changed. Old, unchanged brand values were seen in a new light. Lovers of the brand rubbed their eyes in pleasant surprise. Secret enthusiasts looked forward expectantly to a promising future. The competition found this new departure hard to believe.

The workforce was of decisive importance during this phase, from development to service. They filled the brand values with life and were readily motivated. Their inner resolve to make renewed efforts was supported by dynamic external representation of the brand. Experience at the point of sale has since been fully in keeping with the communicated claims.

Brand management

The brand became a topic at the highest corporate level. This engineer-dominated production and technology company, once likened to a transatlantic steamer, changed into a fast and manoeuvrable catamaran. Previously all knowledge held on the Mercedes-Benz brand was compartmentalized in the communication section, the patent department, the classic section at the museum, the strategic staff departments, corporate PR, and so on. The various perceptions of the brand's importance were not so very different. However, there was no uniform strategy or common objective.

Brand management as a function was firmly installed under marketing and sales at board level, with clearly defined tasks and aims:

Tasks
1. Definition and further development of the Mercedes-Benz brand philosophy/brand strategy (cars, commercial vehicles).

2. Definition of the brand rights of divisions, business units, centres and retail organizations with respect to vehicles, services, cooperative arrangements and licences involving the Mercedes-Benz brand.
3. Responsibility for coordinating the brand interests of Mercedes-Benz in sales.
4. Management of the brand by integrating requirements and defining standards and guidelines.

Aims
- Further development and increase in the value of the Mercedes-Benz brand.
- Protecting the brand from damage, weakening, devaluation.

The brand codex

The second structural level for implementation of the brand positioning, and the strategies derived from it, is the so-called brand 'codex'. As the name indicates, this is the actual rulebook for the use of all brand-characterizing procedures in the three sectors of primary and secondary products, services and customer care, sales and communication. There is a written guideline for each of these areas. However, the decisive aspect is that the established systems and processes are logically derived from the brand positioning and brand strategy, leading to a clear identity logic which can also be checked.

Belief that such a rulebook can be totally clear and consistent would be misplaced, however. Its content is in the hands of numerous responsible personnel and naturally subject to a constant process of adaptation. One thing becomes clear when looking at such a system: a premium brand requires all-round care. In other words, the brand identity must be defined in holistic terms at every point in the value-added chain, starting with design, research and development, via procurement and production to marketing, sales and service. Over the long term, no aspect can be disregarded if the entire structure is not to be put at risk.

Let us look at some of the systems that characterize the Mercedes-Benz identity.

Mercedes-Benz vehicles and their categorization

At Mercedes-Benz, an important step in identity development is to link, and at the same time to distinguish between, the Passenger Car and Commercial Vehicle divisions. For all the differences in their use – commercially-operated trucks, vans and buses on the one hand and the more emotionally driven car world on the other – their historical bond under the same trademark is so strong and natural that it tends to strengthen rather than weaken the brand profile.

At the same time, the brand identity is weighted differently from country to country and region to region, depending on the products produced and sold in these areas. In Brazil and Argentina for example, countries in which Mercedes-Benz commercial vehicles have been produced for many years, the image is heavily influenced by these vehicles and also by corporate activities. On the other hand, an American visiting Europe can be puzzled when encountering a Mercedes-Benz truck or getting into a Mercedes-Benz taxi.

All Mercedes-Benz products are nowadays positioned according to the same basic perception of values, and the projection of this identity in communicative measures is based on the same guidelines.

The horizontal and vertical structure of the passenger car range

We work on the assumption that a hierarchical, vertical structure will always apply in the case of passenger cars, as it is a convention everywhere. This means that the larger a car, the more valuable, powerful and expensive it is considered to be, and vice versa. We also assume that the saloon, as the classical form of car, will basically remain the most cost-effective and most frequently used.

All product developments are in line with this classical policy, which is central to the logic of our approach. It has two major horizontal thrusts: the coupés, convertibles, roadsters and so on, which place less emphasis on rationality and use of space, and at the opposite pole the minivans, MPVs and SUVs with their principal emphasis on space and utility.

Once we had a complete picture of the development path for our car range, the decisive questions arose. What is its heritage? What is its potential? How far can it go? Is it capable of being continuously developed? Can we develop a system of product characteristics which is both typical for the brand and highly distinctive from the competition, while belonging within the overall system?

The Mercedes-Benz model designation system

Traditionally, Mercedes-Benz uses letters and performance figures or engine displacement figures as a model designation system. In addition, certain model series or vehicles have become established as icons, for example the SL as the quintessential sports car or the S-Class as the epitome of the luxury saloon.

These basic elements have been developed into a system which allows the basic saloon configuration to be placed in a hierarchy using a class designation (S-, E-, C-, A-Class), supported by an indicative engine displacement (140–600) or a combination of letters (SL, SLK, CL, CLK) to indicate the less hierarchical but more emotional and alternative vehicle concepts. The term 'class' is only used for communication purposes and is translated into different languages as required, while the vehicles themselves bear the same combination of letters and figures whose position and sequence is precisely defined.

Any new vehicle concept is also positioned according to its place in this system. From which existing model series is it derived? Is this made apparent by the designation? Or is it a new cross-over concept which must be newly positioned and communicated, thereby creating its own class with its own class letter or combination of letters? The system can be both a constraint and a help!

A combination of figures and letters is nowadays the norm for premium cars, as they must be acceptable on a worldwide basis. They cannot rely on culturally fragile emotional interpretations of artificial names which cannot be integrated into a system.

Mercedes-Benz vehicle design

In the motor industry it is without question the products themselves that mainly determine the perceived identity. Everybody sees them daily, and in direct comparison with competitors. They are important because practically all of us use them every day, as a means of transportation and as status symbols. We spend a great deal of money on them and are practically compelled to form an opinion. The consistency and continuity of their design is therefore decisive for the brand image.

For decades, Mercedes-Benz design was seen as rather plain, rational and unexciting, with too little variety. In fact, this tendency was in line with the chosen brand strategy, being aimed at value, durability, a long service life and gradual evolution. At the same time the logic of design consistency was developed – in horizontal terms (across all types of vehicle) and in vertical terms (successive models). Typical branding features such as the radiator, headlights, rear lights, side contours and so on were very carefully updated so that a Mercedes-Benz was always immediately identifiable as such. No other car brand has done this so assiduously over decades.

More dynamism and emotionalism was required when the model range expanded into new segments. The range increased from 5 model series with 12 models in 1990 to 11 model series with around 35 models today, and these had to be distinguishable. For all the liveliness associated with the developments in design characteristics, the logic of a technically innovative, rather matter-of-fact 'German' presence was retained. Ergonomic achievements were never sacrificed in favour of design gimmicks, and branding, especially that of the trademarks themselves, was defined even more rigorously. When assessing the design, one must bear in mind the high value expected of a premium car. With a development time of several years, many more years in production and an even longer lifecycle, the design must remain valid for two whole decades.

The multi-dimensional brand value system forms the background for all developments. It demands the achievement of the basic values of quality, comfort, durability and safety across all model series, but with the trend values permits changing emphasis in the sporty, practical or status-oriented character of a particular model.

The Mercedes-Benz brand design system

Definition of the brand design elements and their use is the most important tool for communication, and therefore for the entire area of representing

50 years and five generations of SLs: there's no better example of
the continuity and dynamism of Mercedes-Benz styling development

and controlling the brand presence. Mercedes-Benz has taken a new approach by realizing its complete brand presence online in the Intranet and Extranet. The so-called Brand Design System (BDS) has been developed to ensure that the brand can be used uniformly worldwide. As a tool for consistent worldwide brand management of the extensive car and commercial vehicle ranges, BDS encompasses all available communication tools and measures and ensures uniformity across the large variety of very different applications.

The system can be used universally. With a mouse click, the users – those responsible for the brand and communications in central departments and the sales organization, as well as external partners such as agencies, suppliers or dealers – are able to find out about the latest developments relating to the presentation of the Mercedes-Benz brand. This means that, in a regular dialogue with the user, all the information, and even reproduction proofs, in line with current standards can be immediately downloaded from the network.

How is the 'Brand Design System' actually structured? What are its constituent parts? In which areas is it used? The BDS is made up of design guidelines created on the basis of the brand positioning. It consists of four different components which are interlinked: the 'brand expression', the 'basic design elements', the 'general design guidelines' and the 'specific design guidelines'.

The 'brand expression' lies at the heart of the system. It describes the positioning, personality and values of the brand, explains its origins and also creates a link with the future (vision). The purpose of the 'brand expression' is to communicate the heritage and personality of the brand in such a way that all those responsible for the brand always think, feel and act in terms of the brand, and communicate this message accordingly.

The 'basic design elements' describe the brand's design foundations. These guidelines precisely specify, among other things, the proportions of the famous trademark, the colours to be used and the type fonts for the different applications. This module ensures that the basic brand design elements are uniformly used in all areas of Mercedes-Benz communication. The 'basic design elements' form the basis for all other BDS modules.

The 'general design guidelines' have a more far-reaching function. They define guidelines for cross-divisional applications. Specifically, this means that they provide the framework for the design of brochures, advertisements, presentations, business documentation, exhibitions and websites. It is particularly the topic of web design that will make a major contribution to ensuring a uniform brand presence in the online media and in all applications, for example, e-commerce and e-customer relationship management.

As the term implies, the 'specific design guidelines' concern specific applications of the two previous components and are, for instance, applicable to a specific corporate unit. One example is 'Mercedes-Benz CharterWay', a fleet management

Mercedes-Benz

The version of the Mercedes-Benz brand and word mark produced specifically for on-screen use

service. CharterWay takes care of all the maintenance, servicing and other aspects of fleet management under the motto 'All you need to do yourself is drive'. The 'specific design guidelines' for CharterWay define how the 'basic design guidelines' and the 'general design guidelines' are used in this special sector. This includes brand colours (colour codes allocated to various different types of contract in addition to those defined for Mercedes-Benz). In addition, the guidelines define the use of the trademark in conjunction with the CharterWay name and prescribe design features for vehicle lettering, signs and labels.

Integrated communications

The beneficial influence of a uniform design system such as BDS can be illustrated by how Mercedes-Benz appears in the media. The layout of Mercedes-Benz advertisements, for instance, has remained virtually unchanged for more than 12 years now. It creates an effect of consistency and stability with its basic colours of grey and silver, the specially developed 'Corporate A' font and a classical structure of illustration, headline and copy. Creative implementation within this framework, occasionally

regarded as somewhat severe, gives rise to creative tension in the interpretation of what is typical for the brand: the mix of trust-inspiring and
calm elements and values with emotions, ingenuity, varied illustrations
and a language expressing a sense of humour. The scope of possibilities
allows dozens of different advertising agencies around the world to create
successful and award-winning campaigns – in the typical Mercedes-Benz
style, but reflecting local trends in implementation.

A significant aspect for a brand which employs autonomous sales
and marketing professionals in all its important international markets is
the integrated planning of those activities that have an impact beyond
national market boundaries, as well as the concentration and shared
use of resources. In this respect also, Mercedes-Benz installed a network
– the Communications and Information System (ComIn) – in which all
of the markets' strategic and conceptual plans as well as their
implementations can be stored online, so that up-to-date and cross-
referenced information on all communication measures is available.

Advertising reflects the global consistency of the Brand Design System
in its layout, but local preferences in the content of words and pictures

This is complemented by data acquired in competition monitoring at headquarters.

The crucial factor for efficiency in an ever more globalized media network is agreement on strategies for combining centralized initiative and control with local implementation. Mercedes-Benz has for years been pursuing a systematic and consistent strategy in sports sponsoring. Alongside direct activities in motor sport, the brand has been promoting tennis, another sport that is present in the media throughout the year and throughout the world. This commitment to tennis is used for customer events at national, regional and local levels in all markets, and even includes the promotion of junior talents. For a credible brand presence, it is crucially important that we position ourselves appropriately. The Mercedes star in the tennis net is an exemplary idea to place the brand right in the middle of the action.

Motor sport and tennis idols are also engaged to support the brand. Figures such as Mika Häkkinen, David Coulthard, Tim Henman and Boris Becker are right at the top in terms of popularity, which complements the credibility of their connections with a premium brand like Mercedes-Benz. Their activities start having a beneficial impact when they succeed in reaching beyond their own medium and play a convincing role as partners of the brand at events or in classical advertising. This impact increases still further if they prove to have a sense of humour, like the team of Boris Becker and Mika Häkkinen, who featured together in several commercials for the C-Class and the A-Class.

The sports sponsoring concept of Mercedes-Benz is complemented by other nationally significant sports, for example golf in the United States and in Asia or football in Germany. However, this is always ruled by the principle of cooperation with top players, top teams and top events to illustrate the leading position of Mercedes-Benz through the choice of partners and media.

Another global-format activity controlled by headquarters has been added to round off sports sponsoring. In 2002 the 'Laureus Sports Awards' will be presented for the third time in Monaco to the world's ten best sportsmen, women and teams. Laureus is a joint venture of Mercedes-Benz and the Richmont Group, which comprises the luxury brands Cartier, Dunhill,

Officine Panarei and others. This award is in the process of becoming the 'Sports Oscar', thereby developing into a media-effective platform for the brands involved.

This branding strategy of Mercedes-Benz, namely of establishing itself in an internationally media-effective lifestyle environment, is also pursued outside the realm of sport. Cooperative ventures are currently being set up with the fashion trade, whose dynamism and creativity are a perfect match for Mercedes-Benz. Activities at the Australian and New York Fashion Shows will shortly be complemented by involvement in the shows in Paris and other cities. It goes without saying that alongside classical advertising and sponsoring, Mercedes-Benz is also endeavouring to bring the brand's character to life in all other important forms of appearance.

Conclusion

Great brands always had to surround their products with stories, customer relationships and the element of legend in order to generate distinguishable added value. Mercedes-Benz has succeeded in doing just that time and again. In the context of today's global market, the positioning of international brands as points of reference, as symbols of belonging to a particular group and as a means of distinguishing oneself plays a more significant role than ever.

The professional use of all the instruments required in this context therefore calls for greater feeling and common sense than ever before. However, the crucial thing for all involved in the process is the fact that the value-oriented attitude of the Mercedes-Benz 'undertaking' has basically remained unchanged for more than 100 years. Gottlieb Daimler is said to have coined the phrase 'The best or nothing'. This refers to the ground-breaking endeavours to achieve product superiority in factual terms, coupled with the determination and the ability to design and coordinate all activities which express the brand logically and consistently: products and services, sales, advertising and sales promotion, press and PR work, social and cultural sponsorship.

The editors comment

Mercedes-Benz is a 'through and through' holistic brand. Built up since the start of motoring history, with a single-minded consistency of purpose and values, the brand reaps the benefit of an approach that is based on the excellence of the products, with a corresponding consistency in all activities. The positioning, including the core values of the brand, pervades the entire scope of the company's operations, now even more sharply defined as the premium brand within the DaimlerChrysler Group portfolio. The stability and consistency of the brand, however, belie the constant monitoring and development which takes place, and which alerted Mercedes-Benz to potential problems, particularly at the beginning of the 1990s. The brand's response was typically holistic, starting with a radical review of its positioning, then innovative new products, and culminating in a vast project to align all brand manifestations. As would be expected, Mercedes-Benz is at the leading edge of brand management as well as of automobile technology, and the brand is being protected and developed more intensively than at any time before. In today's competitive environment, even the best cannot afford to rest on their laurels.

Chapter 6
A Bright Brand Future: Orange

Denise Lewis
Group Director Corporate Affairs, Orange SA

Orange in name and orange in colour

Orange is an exemplary inclusive brand. Without the deep belief in the brand which permeates everything it does, Orange could not have risen from its initial position as last UK entrant to become one of the leading mobile telecommunications companies in the world, with 40 million customers in 20 different markets. However, when it first launched in the UK on 28 April 1994, many wise heads would not have expected it to last out the decade, never mind turn the market on its head and achieve market leadership in just eight years.

Orange was the last player to enter a crowded and unattractive UK mobile market. In the early 1980s two analogue licences had been granted, to Vodafone and Cellnet (jointly owned by BT and Securicor). They were not always allowed to sell directly to consumers. In effect, they sold airtime to a myriad of service providers who in turn sold on airtime packages to users, sometimes via retailers, sometimes directly. Now the mobile phone is ubiquitous, seen as a necessary adjunct to modern western lifestyles. However, less than ten years ago mobile phones were mainly seen as business equipment: they were heavy, clunky and very expensive.

Companies, or individuals, were locked into lengthy contracts, charged connection (and disconnection) fees and a line rental – and then the cost of calls on top. The service providers did not add value, just a percentage onto the wholesale cost of calls. Consumers were not really involved in the choice of who provided the calls, they relied on the retailer or the service provider – and tariffs were difficult to understand, bogged down with complex calculations. The customer was not really taken into account. In 1994, only 4 per cent of homes had mobile phones. Heavy users were business customers, sales executives and company directors.

In the early 1990s, government action was taken that was to shake up mobile communications forever. A White Paper, *Phones on the Move*, allowed Vodafone and Cellnet to introduce digital services. It also offered three new licences, which were won by Microtel, Mercury Personal Communications and Unitel. (The latter two eventually became One2One, now owned by Deutsche Telekom and rebranded as T-Mobile.)

Microtel was bought by Hong Kong-based telecommunications company Hutchison Whampoa. They already had interests in the British market with a paging company and were a service provider connecting customers using Cellnet and Vodafone, so there was already market expertise. However, Microtel had also been involved with a failed mobile communications service, Rabbit, which prejudiced some industry observers against the new brand. For the phones to work, callers had to be in sight of a Rabbit sign, limiting when and where you could make and receive calls.

Who were the competition?

At the beginning of the 1990s consumers did not understand the true potential of the mobile phone. Mobiles were perceived rather as a series of negatives: intrusive in trains and restaurants; confusing tariffs; poor service; patchy coverage; and costly. The current market operators were technology-driven and did not understand their customers' needs. Costs were high as calls were charged on a per minute basis, something the customer was coming to understand was poor value for money. There was an abundance of promotional offers, but they too were confusing.

The new brand would be launching into a market that Cellnet and Vodafone had dominated for nine years. They had fully national networks and millions of customers had already subscribed to their analogue networks. They had also had time to plan how they would block their new competitors, who had to concentrate on building their own networks before market entry. The two market leaders tried to head off the competition by introducing low-user tariffs to attract new customers and had strengthened their positions in the business market.

Mercury One2One took the decision to launch early in 1993 – beating Microtel into the market – by concentrating on building their network in London and the Home Counties. They had a heavy advertising campaign and offered free calls. Vodafone and Cellnet matched their spend on a national basis. The market was hotting up and Microtel was yet to launch.

Who were the customers?

Ten years of a duopoly had created a commodity market in mobile communications. Usage had been prohibitive because existing tariffs had been aimed either at business or at the personal user who had a phone for emergencies and was charged very expensive rates for off-peak calls. So the part of the market with the best potential – personal users – was given little encouragement to use the phones. Microtel spent a long time researching products and customers to understand how they perceived the market. The big users were business, but the huge potential lay in persuading consumers to buy phones for personal use.

Launching the new brand

While setting up a national network was the priority for Microtel, the company also realized that it would have to rewrite the rule book if it was to make an impression on a market where it would be the fourth entrant.

The orange launch campaign of April 1994 featured a 'floating baby' to signal brand values

In May 1993, starting with the premise that 'a brand is a promise delivered', a team was set up to develop a set of values and a brand proposition that would engage the consumer emotionally while delivering tangible benefits. The difference about the Microtel team was that they were totally consumer-centric. The business was developed with the customer in mind, whether it was product offer or service. The team was charged with:

- choosing a new name
- developing the values, vision and philosophy
- creating a new brand – a new way of doing business
- creating advertising and promotional tools for launch.

The name

Microtel was not a name that the team felt would take the brand forward to the twenty-first century. It was technology based, rather than forward looking, and it was not aspirational. Working with the core brand proposition and composite idea, a shortlist of names was created, including Pecan, Gemini, Egg, Miron and, of course, Orange.

'Orange' was felt to be the word that best represented what the planned brand would become, with its connotations of optimism, fun and freedom. Market research indicated that people found the name distinctive and friendly, extrovert, modern and powerful. It was placed in the same categories as Virgin, Sainsburys, McDonald's and Sony as being authoritative and desirable.

There were of course concerns that, while the company appreciated the benefits of owning such a warm and friendly word in the telecommunications market, the name would not be taken seriously. However, there were precedents, and the name 'Apple' had not held back that very successful computer firm. While the name did not have connections with 'communications' or 'technology', the team believed this to be a positive rather than a negative.

The simple new name was matched with a clean and simple identity: an orange square with the word 'orange' written in a simple, exclusive, lowercase white font – simple yet distinctive and the now unmistakable strapline – 'the future's bright, the future's Orange.'

The values and brand proposition

Once the name and identity were in existence, further research was commissioned among personal and business customers. They were asked their views about the name, proposition, colour, logo, and benefits to customers. Brainstorming by the launch team refined the core brand proposition to a composite of three ideas: my world, manager, my friend. The composite idea was 'It's my life.' This led to a definitive set of Orange brand values. The values identified were very simple: refreshing, honest, dynamic and friendly:

- **Refreshing.** Orange is bright and cheerful. Orange aims to liberate people from the constraints of yesterday's technology, providing them with user-friendly products and services, wherever, whenever and however they want to use them.
- **Honest.** Orange is completely transparent with clear communications that cut through confusion. Straightforward. Orange makes things easier by using simple language and no jargon.
- **Dynamic.** Orange is continually striving to be innovative and dynamic.
- **Friendly.** Orange is a brand that you can trust.

Orange is perhaps unusual in that the values and brand proposition that were developed for launch are still valid and adhered to today. It is these values that have set Orange apart: not just the fact that it has them, but that the company lives them. Orange believes its brand humanizes its products and services. The brand values apply not only to our relationship with our customers, but also inform our behaviour as a company towards our suppliers, our partners and our colleagues.

The brand vision was to create a better future, where people can communicate and access information wherever, whenever and however they wish. Orange aimed to revolutionize mobile telephony and eliminate confusion by making it easy to use a mobile phone. It created a new space in the mobile market and called it 'wirefree'. We realized the potential that wire-free technology could have in the future and did not want to be put in the same box as our competitors. We created 'wirefree' (which we trademarked) as a launchpad for a flexible future – communications no longer limited by wire, and eventually not limited to voice but encompassing e-mail, text, video, banking, news content and so much more. Orange succeeded by differentiating itself from the competition:

- It was the first mobile company to talk to its customers in a clear and unambiguous manner. Communications were simple to understand.
- Calls were to be charged by the second, instantly avoiding the rip-off charges levied by competitors. Each contract involved a care package, offering unrivalled customer service and 24-hour replacement.
- It introduced innovations such as simple 'Talk Plan' tariffs that offered real value for money, caller ID, itemized billing free of charge, and direct customer relationships.

Creating the brand

The launch of Orange is well documented as being one of the most unusual and innovative campaigns in the UK. It won many awards and created a lot of controversy at the time. More importantly, it created awareness of the brand very quickly, which was essential given that it was entering the market a long way behind the other three major players.

Perhaps the strongest and most memorable element was the strapline Orange's then advertising agency developed: 'The future's bright. The future's Orange.' The brand was inextricably linked to the future and a promise that the company would help customers manage that future. People are attracted to new technological developments but also distrust them. They looked to Orange to help them find their way through it. The strapline was well accepted by consumers and has become one of the most successful in advertising history.

The Orange brand strategy was not a cautious one. The company knew that it would have to get it right first time, but was still prepared to take risks. Research had shown that consumers had an ambivalent attitude to mobile phones. They did not want to be associated with the vulgarity or nuisance factor. Nor did they wish to become a prisoner of technology. However, they agreed with all the benefits that suppliers told them mobile telephony would bring. It also showed that their attitude towards Vodafone and Cellnet left plenty of room for a competitor who could speak to consumers in their own language and offer them benefits they understood. Above all, the Orange team's research suggested that they should avoid the type of advertising that was technology or price-based.

As a result, Orange took the bold decision that mobile phones should not appear in any of its advertising. Instead its communications focused upon the benefits that people would derive from the mobile phone. In a complex and confusing market, it brought clarity. In a technology-driven market, which at the time seemed to have few new services to offer, it brought innovation.

Oftel (the UK's telephone regulatory body) placed Orange first in its 1998 Best Performance survey. The 'Top Dog' campaign celebrated this success

As Cellnet and Vodafone had been focusing on consumer costs for the previous ten years, Orange avoided it. Instead its intention was to create a strong and vibrant brand identity that would give people the confidence to trust its pricing structures. It was not interested in competing in a commodity market.

In terms of profiling the customer, Orange identified a type rather than a

'Orange's digital technology means that your call will always get through': a campaign from 1995

demographic group. These were the 'independents' who made choices for themselves and would appreciate the iconic nature of Orange's communications.

Talk, listen, laugh, cry

The Orange values shaped the advertising campaign. On 28 April 1994, Orange was officially launched and giant teaser posters with the words 'Talk', 'Listen', 'Laugh' and 'Cry' covered London. The posters were black and contained only the one word, the Orange logo and the strapline. For those who saw them for the first time, there was no indication that the ads were for a mobile phone company. They were imposing, difficult to miss and set the style for Orange's poster advertising for many years. More explanatory ads appeared in the press and on television, but again these concentrated on benefits, not price or technology.

Spring was not traditionally a strong selling period for mobile phone services, but it was the earliest date the brand could be launched. The actual date was chosen on the basis of positive feng shui, important to its then Hong Kong Chinese parent company.

Initially, consumers were confused by the advertising: 60 per cent on the first Millward Brown tracking study six weeks after launch did not understand the campaign. However, the intention was to build awareness not instant sales, so the company did not waiver from its strategy. It was creating an iconic brand and the mystique also made it interesting.

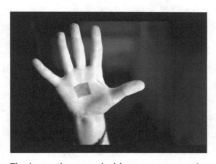

The instantly recognizable orange square in an advertisement for Orange.net mobile internet services

Over the next few years, Orange ran saturation campaigns. The posters introduced each new theme; television communicated core benefits and press provided detailed messages. The timing of campaigns was different from competitors who tended to advertise during the three month run up to Christmas. Orange educated the market in the middle of the year, taking advantage of cheaper advertising rates and establishing brand credentials that were not based on price. Also, as competitors were not advertising, Orange had 100 per cent share of the media space.

During the Christmas period, sales were encouraged with short-term market messages on the back of strong brand awareness. Orange managed to successfully convey detailed product information such as per second billing and text messaging, and at the same time create a very powerful, well understood brand image.

The synergy created between the brand identity and the advertising undoubtedly contributed to the brand's success. The identity was the framework for the press and poster advertising, and it was used consistently in all consumer material, direct mail and promotions. All the agencies understood and subscribed to the need to be truly consistent in both image and content. Orange advertising has continued to be stylish and to communicate a clear proposition. The approach is aspirational but with appeal to a broad mass market.

Orange's customer magazine

Sponsorship also played an important role from the early days. The strategy was to use this technique to build brand awareness among key potential users. Orange did not want to replicate the sports sponsorships chosen by its competitors, instead pursuing other areas of customer interest: literature, film, education and music. Its approach

Talk, the magazine for Orange's employees in the UK

was to look at each area, highlight where the funding gap was, then decide how that arena could be used as a differentiator. For example, there were other literature prizes, but the Orange prize for fiction was the first for female authors. Orange is now one of the largest sponsors of the arts in Europe.

The only diversion from this strategy came in 2000 when Orange looked to build brand awareness on a global scale and wanted a medium that would deliver this quickly. We audited sports properties and the overwhelming winner was Formula One motor racing. It has a massive following and is one of the most dynamic sports, which showcases emerging technologies. In looking at the opportunities available within motor racing, we did adhere to our original strategy: choosing the Arrows team, the underfunded underdog. While they may not yet have delivered winners, our sponsorship records the second highest consumer awareness, after Ferrari – at a considerably lower cost.

Growing the company

By the end of 1995, the Orange customer base had more than doubled to 785,000 from 397,000 at the end of 1994. The structure of the company was also to change radically, with an IPO, two acquisitions and the expansion from a solely UK business to a multi-national corporate entity. In 1996 Orange plc underwent its first initial public offering, with the shares being listed on the London and Nasdaq markets on 2 April. With a valuation of £2.4 billion, Orange plc became the youngest company to enter the FTSE-100.

In July 1997 the company reached its first milestone, clocking up its one millionth customer. Orange plc was named the best performing share in 1998, based on companies listed on the FTSE-100 throughout the year.

In June 1999 Orange won the NatWest/Sunday Times Business Enterprise Award, which described Orange as 'one of the outstanding business success stories of the past few years' and the Orange story as one of 'courageous vision and commitment to the long-running potential of mobile telecoms'.

Having established a strong presence in the UK, Orange naturally looked abroad for markets where it could begin its international expansion. Orange Communications SA was awarded a GSM 1800 licence in Switzerland in 1998 and launched its service on 29 June 1999. Twelve months after launch as Switzerland's third network, Orange Communications SA took the number two position with a market share of 17 per cent and the biggest customer growth.

By the end of 1999, Orange had licensed its brand to operators in Hong Kong, Australia, Israel and India. Orange was launched in Hong Kong in September 1998, and went from fourth to first in the market within six months. In Israel, Orange gained over 400,000 customers in its first year, and is recognized as the biggest brand in the country.

In October 1999, Mannesmann AG (the majority shareholder in one of the leading mobile operators in Germany) announced the acquisition of Orange plc for £19.8 billion. The offer was completed in February 2000 and Orange was delisted from the London and Nasdaq stock exchanges. During this time Mannesmann itself was bought by Vodafone, a deal approved by the European Commission subject to an undertaking from Vodafone to divest Orange plc. Subsequently, in August 2000, France Telecom acquired Orange plc from Vodafone for a total consideration of £25.1 billion. Orange plc's wirefree interests were merged with the majority of those of France Telecom to form the new Orange SA group.

On 13 February 2001, Orange SA was floated on the EuroNext Paris. Despite the changes in ownership, Orange continued to concentrate on providing the best service to its customers. In May 2001, for the fourth consecutive year, Orange UK was ranked number one in JD Power and Associates UK Mobile Customer Satisfaction Study.

At the end of December 2001, Orange had more than 39 million subscribers with controlled interests in France, UK, Belgium, the Netherlands, Switzerland, Romania, Denmark, Slovakia, Sweden, Ivory Coast, Dominican Republic, Cameroon, Botswana and Madagascar. Orange also has minority interests in Italy, Germany, Portugal, Austria, Thailand and Mumbai (India).

In May 2001, Orange SA was admitted to the CAC40, France's top 40 companies ranked by market capitalization.

Keeping the brand Orange

The Orange brand survived not only its purchase and sale by a German company, but also its current ownership by a French company. In fact it not only survived, but has come to be the dominant brand in the former France Telecom group. Jean-François Pontal, Orange CEO, said, 'France Telecom recognized the Orange brand had the credibility to become the first truly global communications brand. It was unique in its sector and represented a company that had successfully communicated a vision of the future that was new and inspiring, which transformed the customer's experience of mobile communications and created enormous shareholder value.'

Guiding principles
Orange has developed Ten Guiding Principles for Global Brand Management, which demonstrate why the brand has achieved such success:

1. Understand that a brand is more than skin deep

This is our definition of holistic branding. Orange is more than a logo. It is how we behave, our ethos, our attitude and way of doing business – and the lifeblood of our company.

As we take Orange out to the world, whether it is re-branding all 20 of France Telecom's existing mobile services or franchising the brand to like-minded operators, we are not just exporting the Orange badge, we are exporting the Orange way of doing business.

The medium and message of all sorts of promotional material is in line with Orange's brand values

2. The brand as differentiator

Being the fourth brand into the UK marketplace, we were aware from the beginning that we had to innovate to differentiate. A 'me too' strategy would not attract customers and, more importantly, make that important breakthrough in developing the market and releasing the huge potential in personal use.

Our vision was based on a very simple principle: to create a better future, where people can communicate and access information wherever, whenever and however they wish. We aimed to revolutionize mobile telephony and to eliminate confusion by making it easy to use a mobile phone. We have stayed firmly with the original proposition that customers do not care about networks, standards or systems. They simply want to enjoy products and services that are easy to use and enable them to live their lives better.

This does not mean that we ignore the fundamentals. We focus on:

- network quality and performance
- excellent customer service and care
- creating value for customers, employees and shareholders.

3. Orange on the inside

Our guiding principle is that we do not put our brand on the outside of our controlled operations until it is living and breathing on the inside. So far in 2002 we have already rebranded Thailand, Slovakia and Romania. The Ivory Coast, Cameroon and Poland are also earmarked for this year, but no country becomes Orange until it is able to demonstrate that it has satisfied our quality standards.

In so doing, we are avoiding the mistakes that many companies make as they expand from their base: allowing the brand to lose its core identity and values in an attempt to appease local viewpoints. We have a global vision for the brand which is very much the same as when it was launched into the UK eight years ago.

As a service industry, our employees are an integral part of the brand. To ensure that our employees truly 'speak Orange', we have developed in-depth induction processes that cover both individuals and new businesses. Everyone from a new CEO to a new customer service representative goes through it. It explains in detail our values, philosophy, vision and how these translate into business. It inspires passion in our employees – a passion that can't be bought or incentivized.

When we recruit we look for a certain kind of attitude as much as skills or qualifications. We search for the right attitude to match the brand: positive thinking, adaptability and the readiness to take up a challenge. The passion that Orange employees have for their brand brings considerable, tangible benefits. The performance of our Customer Communication Centres is enhanced because people are immersed in the ethos of Orange. This takes many forms, such as positive slogans on the desk and the new Aromatherapy room that has fragrances to match each of the core values. Throughout the building, colleagues are surrounded by examples of the Orange ethos. We believe in looking after our employees in the same way that we want them to look after our customers.

Having visited our Tyneside Customer Communications Centre in the UK, a reporter for the *Guardian* wrote, 'For a manager, this is the perfect workforce. Enthusiastic, intelligent, resourceful and hardworking, and with an uncynical faith hard to match in any other area of life outside the workplace: political parties and churches used to inspire this kind of commitment. They remain "passionately" loyal to the brand. Once your workforce is emotionally attached to the brand, they will follow it anywhere.'

4. Don't mess with the identity

We have invested a lot of time and money in creating an identity which has proven to work for Orange. So we also spend a lot of time in ensuring that it does not become diluted or shifted away from our guiding principles as we expand our business.

The essence of our brand is a bright human future, and everything we do is couched in the language, activity and optimism that reflect that ambition. So as we re-brand, some fundamentals are sacrosanct and consistency is imperative. People's experience of the brand and what it represents must be the same wherever they are in the world, the same values and also the same corporate identity: the Orange square; the typeface; the vocabulary; the colours; the famous strapline. All must be replicated precisely and sensitively. We are committed to delivering the same consumer experience around the world. This is what empowers the brand.

5. Understand the framework

While we impose consistency on the fundamentals of the business, we also encourage flexibility in how the brand is articulated. It must fit in with the local environment. Therefore we need to study and understand it and take on board the experience of our local operators, to enable the brand to leverage the local market dynamics.

These first five principles are very generic and could be applied to any business. The next five are specific to Orange and support the values that are at the heart of our business.

6. Establish the brand values

One of the reasons for the success of the Orange brand has been its consistent adherence to the values which were created when the brand was launched. They underpin our business. What sets us apart is not that we have these values, but that we live them.

The delivery of our promise to our customers is our goal every minute of the day. Without this commitment, we would not be able to achieve our other goals of business growth and positive returns for stakeholders. To ensure that new markets understand our passion for Orange, we have created Centres of Excellence from every discipline across the group. The best managers are put into countries as part of the induction process to ensure that the Orange philosophy is understood and adopted quickly and correctly.

7. The flexible brand

From the beginning there was a bigger vision for Orange than a wirefree device for people to speak to each other. So we set ourselves apart from the rest of the industry by maintaining communications messages that did not restrict us. We have established a strong brand that can retain its original character and yet still look ahead and change. It is flexible enough to evolve to the ever-changing needs of our customers. Our ultimate goal is to be a global life services brand – and there is nothing in our current or past brand communications that could create a confusion in consumers' minds about this.

8. Constant and consistent articulation of our vision

We consistently articulate our vision and, more importantly, it is part of our culture. Within Orange, it is a living, breathing narrative, which constantly challenges the norm and redefines its terms of reference.

Orange has a cool, iconic appeal to customers, which is able to cross borders and has avoided the disillusionment which many people feel about some of the major multi-national brands. Protecting this trust will be essential for the future, and Orange is embarking on a major corporate social responsibility review which involves auditing every aspect of the company's community, ethical and social status. From this will come embedded policies covering fundamental principles of behaviour and a programme of action.

9. Listening to our customers

The capacity to learn and grow is as fundamental to success as the capacity to deliver service. Our organization is keenly aware of the issues of our customers, from sitting and listening to customer care staff to sculpting a strategic framework for our business which is focused on how to engage and satisfy our existing and future customers.

10. Living the brand

At Orange we truly live the brand – our brand is our central business discipline. It defines what we are as a company, how we relate to our people and what we bring to customers. By so doing we have created one of the most credible brands in the world.

The future's bright

So where next for Orange? The brand has achieved iconic status in its mature markets and is making rapid inroads around the world. Orange SA is one of the world's leading communications companies. Today, Orange is number one in the UK (in terms of active customers) and France and, in terms of footprint, the second largest mobile operator in Europe. Orange group companies have been awarded next generation (UMTS) licences in the UK, the Netherlands, Germany, Italy, Austria, Sweden, Switzerland, Portugal, Belgium and France.

While Orange started largely as a personal use brand, its parent France Telecom dominates the business market in France so with the benefit of its expertise, Orange will be challenging the established business brands in the near future. It is ideally placed to take advantage of new developments in mobile communications and telephony and help consumers take part in the lifestyle and information revolutions. People will be communicating via text, voice and video using their phone, but the phone itself will become much more than a communication device. It will enable a myriad of different services such as mobile-payment, access to film archives and even home security.

We will be offering these life services in conjunction with other best in breed brands so that our customers can access and download what they need without being tied to a desk or a computer. It is important that when these developments arrive, consumers can place such trust in Orange that they will be happy for us to look after their money or their home, and that they can totally accept that we will be introducing them to new ways of managing their lives.

The editors comment

The Orange brand is now such a familiar part of our lives that it is easy to overlook the extraordinary speed and assurance with which it has gained its ubiquity. The key to this success, without any doubt, is the inclusive nature of the brand. As Denise Lewis points out, the brand beliefs permeate every aspect of Orange's thinking and doing. The result is a homogeneity, and consequent strength, of all dimensions from the performance of the service, through the style of the communications to the behaviour of the company and its employees. Launching into a market where established competition seemed invincible, Orange sought to understand, then exceed, customer expectations. The first priority was a set of values and a brand proposition. Everything else followed from this and was guided by the belief that 'a brand is a promise delivered'. Orange is a fine example of a holistic approach to branding, and demonstrates the success achievable when all dimensions and aspects are aligned with a powerful, customer-oriented vision.

Chapter 7
Changing Preconceptions: BUPA

Peter Smythe
Head of Brand Management, BUPA

BUPA (a contraction of British United Provident Association) has a reputation as a pioneer of private health care. BUPA is the largest organization of its kind in the UK, and has an annual turnover of some £2 billion. Its surplus before tax in the year 2000 was £65.4 million. BUPA's status as a provident association means that it does not have shareholders and ploughs back all profits for the benefit of its customers.

For a number of years, the organization has been diversifying from health insurance into hospitals, health screening, care homes and other health and care services. Today, less than half its income is derived from its health insurance activities. But for the vast majority of the UK audience, perceptions of BUPA remained stuck in the health insurance box. A holistic approach to change management and communications was required if BUPA was to break out of that box, and be reborn as a provider of a wide range of health and care services.

So it embarked on a brand repositioning programme, the like of which the company had not seen in its 55 years of existence. The result would be the transformation of what was seen as essentially a single-product company into one that spanned a number of areas. The new BUPA would be seen not only as having a wider base, but also as responsive to, and providing for, a customer's lifetime health and care needs.

The repositioning operated at many levels and was introduced throughout the business in an inclusive and employee-oriented way. The outcome was an organization embracing a new set of values, imbued with qualities of service, individual accessibility, respect and expertise.

Comparisons with the dramatic changes introduced to service standards in retailing are inescapable and apt.

BUPA's services had to be revamped dramatically to enable it to re-present itself as a broad-based provider of innovative and customer-centred services. For example, the company re-engineered its well-known health insurance offering to meet carefully researched customer needs and expectations. It produced some innovations, to enable the company to cover the expense of medical care for specified conditions from which the customer was already suffering, a move which was hailed as both innovative and imaginative. It instituted many other changes to the brand positioning of its hospital, health assessment and care homes services, as we shall describe. Two years of concentrated self-assessment and market analysis were required before it was prepared to go public with the wide and ambitious vision it had set itself. Only after that period of assessment was accomplished would it express to the outside world the new consumer proposition.

The strapline encapsulating the change was as powerful as the change itself: 'the personal health service'. The strength of the statement was a measure of BUPA's commitment to an individualized service and identification with a comprehensive range of services rather than its historic focus on medical insurance.

The brand repositioning represents perhaps the last step in a fundamental transition. The one-time post-war provider of private medicine to the

BUPA's repositioning statement, encapsulated within the logotype

few who could afford it in an era of austerity is now a service organization capable of building on its already market-leading position in the twenty-first century. BUPA's repositioning enabled it to stand as a confident organization, reasserting its leadership in UK private health care provision.

Route to a transformation

The route to this cultural and structural transformation was complex: it involved a repositioning of the company through a guiding vision, a launch of new products, a coordinated internal communications programme for staff, an advertising push on television and integrated product marketing campaigns.

To establish such fundamental change within an organization known by staff and public alike for its health insurance required deep introspection. No part of the company's brand was left untouched as BUPA sought to sell its range convincingly to a public whose perceptions of its brand were entrenched in health insurance. This completely holistic brand repositioning involved staff, customers and the wider public. Competitors quickly saw that BUPA was cutting out for itself a new market position which would challenge existing assumptions.

Research findings point the way

The transformation was born out of a piece of quantitative market research at the end of 1998, which had some sobering news for the company. First, it confirmed that the market for its core business of private medical insurance (PMI) was in long-term decline and unlikely to grow again substantially. Over four years, the number of subscribers had fallen by 1 per cent to just below 3.5 million, covering 6.4 million people or approximately 11 per cent of the adult population of the UK. The outlook was no more promising. At the same time, its position as market leader was facing growing competition from those who saw PMI potentially as a commodity product.

Brand preference for BUPA was also dropping sharply. Whereas over 40 per cent of those who said that they might buy PMI had claimed they were most likely to choose BUPA during 1997, the number was only 32 per cent by the end of 1998. Reduced advertising support had also led to a drop in the brand's profile, which had fallen to its lowest level for several years. Amongst the adult population, BUPA's level of spontaneous awareness, which in the mid-1990s had been around 75 per cent, had fallen to 65 per cent. BUPA was believed to be expensive, but many potential customers also excluded themselves from BUPA on moral grounds. BUPA was seen by some as a rather anti-social way of bypassing the UK's National Health Service, the state-owned medical service which is free to all UK citizens at the point of entry.

Top management commitment

The challenge to a new senior management and marketing team was clear. It had to reinvigorate the brand, broaden the appeal of the organization's services to a wider range of people, or risk watching the company stagnate. One early and vital step taken by the new management was to change its policy towards the brand budget and view it as an asset requiring consistent investment. Under the new management, the brand budget was ring-fenced in order to improve long-term performance.

It was clear that repositioning was necessary, but the new position could not be achieved solely through external brand building. Internally, new core values would have to be identified and agreed. Services would have to be enhanced. And this would all be driven by a new vision that inspired and united the organization. BUPA had to be seen not as a specialist health insurer for the few who could afford it (or whose employers paid for it), but as a broad-based provider of health and care for the many, who would find it accessible and responsive. This was the only way forward.

From insurance to all-round care

This meant positioning the company as the first choice for health and care rather than the first choice for health insurance. BUPA put it like this: we want to be a health and care company that also provides insurance rather than a health insurance company that also happens to offer health and care.

For BUPA to be repositioned in consumers' minds, it had to start behaving differently both internally and externally. There were three main areas for attention:

- The prevailing image of BUPA as a profit-oriented business had to be tempered by an increase in awareness of its 'provident' nature (that is, no shareholders and all money retained in the business for the benefit of its customers) and people-oriented status.
- The prevailing image had to move from being seen as an alternative, or even adversary, to the UK's National Health Service, to being complementary to it.
- It also had to move from being seen as expensive and exclusive, to being 'for me' and accessible.

Brand-stretching, a new competence

The repositioning was not just about addressing the negative perceptions, it was also forward-looking. Through a commitment to 'brand stretching', BUPA sought to spread its authority in the PMI sector to a much larger range of products in a market it prefers to call 'health and care', rather than 'healthcare'. In the course of this expansion of brand equity, it has arguably pioneered a new competence, where no one else could come close on range and expertise.

Its position in the health and care market was to be established by drawing on values of caring and individual concern, rather than merely of financial provision. This gave rise to a project to determine a new motivating vision for the organization. Six months of discussions with senior people in each of BUPA's divisions resulted in universal agreement to eight words: 'taking care of the lives in our hands'.

Products repositioning is key

The product range was imaginatively enhanced and branded to embrace the new BUPA values. Four services were given particular attention: BUPA hospitals; medical insurance with the launch of BUPA Heartbeat; BUPA care homes; and BUPA health assessment (from the BUPA Wellness division).

BUPA's product logotypes

BUPA hospitals

BUPA's hospitals were repositioned with an individualist ethic embodied in a proposition called 'fixed price care'. The task was to differentiate the hospitals on the personal nature of the service and to inform people that they were open to all, not just BUPA members. The fixed-price package determines the cost of treatment before it is started, so removing the anxiety that the meter is running if the treatment or recovery takes longer than expected. It also enabled BUPA to broaden the market beyond the insured population to those individuals prepared to pay for their own treatment.

BUPA Heartbeat

The same spirit of reassurance and customer orientation was evident in the reworking of its medical insurance package. Called BUPA Heartbeat, this broke new ground in two directions: first, it offered to cover some existing conditions from which the patient was already suffering; second, the price could be tailored more closely to the customer's needs.

The company also sought to overcome some of the political prejudices against private medical insurance by emphasizing BUPA's own provident status. The fact that any profit is reinvested in more health and care facilities comforts potential purchasers, and can be the decisive differentiator from the range of commercial companies that have entered the health insurance market. Research has shown that, at the point of purchase, the sense that the customer is going to an organization that does not set out to deliver profits to shareholders as a result of people's ill health can be helpful in decision making.

BUPA care homes
BUPA's presence in care homes is substantial. It leads the market with over 230 homes serving some 15,000 customers, but awareness of them was very low. The care homes represented an important element in the ability to position BUPA as a broad-ranging health and care organization. The task here was to raise awareness of care homes but in a way that was sensitive to the concerns of the elderly.

BUPA Wellness
BUPA Wellness was the new name for the division responsible for BUPA's wide range of health maintenance services such as health assessment and occupational health. It has centres all round the UK. It was expanding rapidly through the acquisition of corporate health services, particularly in the London area. These services bring a lot to the brand, differentiating it as concerned about keeping people well, not just treating them when they are ill, and they were to be an important feature of the repositioning campaign.

Changing staff attitudes: the 'One Life' programme
While BUPA was reappraising its product line, it also embarked on a programme to engage staff. It was recognized that people experience the brand through the staff, so their commitment to and belief in the brand were vital. They have the power to make the difference. The company's vehicle was a programme called 'One Life'. BUPA wanted to expose each member of its staff to the new vision in a day-long programme. A follow-up programme for managers was called 'Leading One Life'.

Service-driven and particularly care-driven businesses thrive when people harness their own experiences to their role as carers, and the 'One Life' programme aimed to demonstrate BUPA's commitment to this principle. Well structured programmes which are aligned to the corporate vision and strategy play a key role. They are not, however, one-off events designed to indoctrinate those attending with the company line, but rather sustained efforts to enable people to discover how they can make their own individual contributions to delivering customer-focused service, developing effective leadership skills and strengthening the core values at the heart of an organization's culture.

During periods of economic uncertainty, it would be easy to neglect such development, but BUPA realized that there is no worse time to risk employee motivation than during difficult economic periods. At such times, they rely on their staff more than ever to produce quality outcomes.

Individualism at the hub of the message

The 'One Life' programme recognized that if BUPA treated its own staff as individuals, they would respond by seeing their customers as individuals. The 'One Life' motif was imbued with the conviction that each individual has only one life, that each life is different and unique, and that it is quite acceptable, indeed positively desirable, for people to behave differently and according to their own inner truths.

The message that BUPA regarded each life as important, together with its mission of caring for life, was distilled into a new internal vision designed to inspire the whole organization: 'taking care of the lives in our hands'. And it was widely disseminated through internal communications material as well as at the 'One Life' day meetings.

To encourage a sense of empowerment, BUPA made every effort to break down the barriers between home, where individuals feel comfortable expressing themselves, and work, where they typically feel inhibited. So staff were invited to dress as they wished for the day, and be prepared to demonstrate a hobby of their choosing. Harmony and good feeling were important for the event to be successful, and BUPA put great effort into selecting the cross-section of individuals attending each day's event. Diverse personalities and a spread of ages were brought together on each occasion. An atmosphere conducive to relaxation and sharing was encouraged, allowing staff to show competences they usually showed only outside the workplace.

Those attending came away with the sense of a diverse organization in which individualism and caring are valued. The message they absorbed was that, if people were able to accept and value the diversity of their colleagues, they would see their own customers as individuals, listen to their very different needs and then tailor services accordingly.

More than 12,000 people attended the 'One Life' programmes, which were held at four centres over six months. Care had to be taken to keep BUPA's services running at their normal high levels of operational efficiency while staff were attending the course, so these one-day sessions were a major logistical exercise in themselves. The conclusion from the 'One Life' programmes was that the energy, ideas and dedication of all employees could indeed be better harnessed. They showed how, in many cases, simple ideas put forward by employees could lead directly to improvements in working practices and customer service.

An introduction for managers: 'Leading One Life'
Following a successful delivery of 'One Life' programmes to staff, a separate programme called 'Leading One Life' was presented to over 1,000 managers. This sought to encourage BUPA's senior staff to create a more caring culture among employees and think carefully about harnessing the effort and energy of each individual in their teams, whilst rewarding and celebrating dedication and achievement.

Participants in the 'Leading One Life' programme were drawn from across the business, including hospitals, care homes, insurance and occupational health. They represented all functional areas and reflected the diversity of BUPA's people and businesses. The 'Leading One Life' programme has played an important part in bringing together a diverse and internationally spread organization to adopt a common vision.

The programme challenged participants to ask what they could bring to the workplace to support colleagues or customers and understand their concerns. They were also required to think seriously about the implications of BUPA's encouragement of the development of the individual. In the health and care sector, customers need support in moments of crisis, whether making an insurance claim, arranging an operation, seeking care for an elderly relative or handing over a precious child to a nursery. Four million people put their lives in BUPA's hands and the company has to be there for them. The 'Leading One Life' programme helped staff to view all customers as individuals and deliver the best possible care.

'One Life' awards

Management development really begins when people leave the workshop setting and return to their teams, taking responsibility for creating a more customer-focused organization. Over the past year, 1,700 ideas have been put forward by BUPA's people for 'One Life' Awards, to encourage innovation in delivering service, both internally and externally. Adoption rates are as high as 40 percent and the ideas that have been implemented include a health line for women facing surgery for breast cancer, an activities booklet to prepare children for being admitted into hospital and even a dashboard card system designed to prevent 'parking rage' in a congested staff car park.

The awards needed to be able to recognize and reward people at every level of the workforce. Effective internal communications, including in-house newspapers and the Intranet, keep the momentum going. Employee surveys and regular 360 degree feedback for all managers provide benchmarks for standards of leadership and management practice. BUPA's Service Organization Profile (SOP), in which all employees take part, measures critical elements that influence employee satisfaction, including leadership, group climate and group tension, role overload and role ambiguity, job satisfaction and career development.

Customer satisfaction surveys indicate consistency in quality and service levels in all customer groups. But, above all, the contribution of training and development is reflected in corporate growth and increased profits.

Impact on profits

The 'Leading One Life' and 'One Life' schemes are believed to have contributed to BUPA's increase in profits over the past two years. This is good news for any commercial organization but for BUPA, a provident association with no shareholders, the effect of improved profits is to allow it to reinvest increasing amounts in health and care services and continually improve service delivery to customers.

Understanding people, and what drives and enthuses them, is essential in a customer-focused business. A commitment to the personal development of each employee yields job satisfaction, which in turn improves customer service and customer satisfaction, the attainment of best practice and long-term corporate success. Only after the internal communications programme was in place to help staff deliver the brand promise would BUPA contemplate the external brand-building programme.

Marketing objectives

Repositioning the brand would be driven by the development and launch of a new advertising campaign. The previous 'Amazing' campaign had already won considerable acclaim, but now BUPA wanted to home in on the product range and emphasize its wide range of competences in the health and care sectors. The requirements of the new marketing approach were stated in the pitch brief given to communication agencies: these were to:

- create a brand expression that could unite the range, raise awareness of BUPA's services beyond PMI and support the launch of innovative new services
- provide a platform to appeal to a wider audience and make the brand appear more accessible
- differentiate the BUPA PMI proposition in the face of aggressive new entrants that are rapidly turning it into a commodity market where price is the only discriminator.

The priority was to shift consumer awareness and understanding of the brand to establish its new positioning.

Developing a communications solution

A new 'brand model' was developed to reposition the brand, to ensure that appropriate weight was given to each of its messages, and most impor-tantly, that the different values asserted for the new BUPA were consistent with the new vision to become 'the personal health service'. The advertising campaign would build on the highly successful 'Amazing' campaign (strapline: 'You're amazing. We want you to stay that way') which had established BUPA's brand stature but not sought to advance awareness of specific services. Agencies were given a very different brief for the new campaign. The various services would be used as exemplars of the brand in action in order to project the core values.

The development of a new BUPA personality was critical to the campaign. It needed to present BUPA as more human, caring and expert. The image of masculine authority would need to be softened, while more feminine values of caring and concern would be introduced. By blending the masculine values of the doctor with the feminine values of the nurse, BUPA would retain its former reputation for authority and medical expertise while acquiring values of care and nurturing necessary for a company which looks after the old and sick, young and well.

New brand proposition

A period of intense research and testing resulted in the creation of a 'brand temple' model. At the base of the temple are the 'functional' needs of the consumer like 'choice', 'services tailored to my needs', 'accessible services'. The next level up deals with the consumer's emotional needs, like 'I want to be kept as well as I can be', 'I want to be in control of my health', 'I need reassurance'. On this were built the product pillars as exemplars of the brand in action. Through the products would emerge the core values and the brand personality, all of which was expressed in the brand essence: the personal health service, which formed the roof of the temple. It was important that this was rooted in something that would make powerful sense to consumers and prove a credible revision of BUPA's role.

A persuasive tool

Research had made clear the extent of the lack of knowledge about the organization. BUPA realized they needed to give people some 'new news' to force them to confront and overturn some of their assumptions about the organization. Specific areas of the business required support, with stories relevant to their particular audience segments. But the vital point was to ensure that each of these also contributed to a wider understanding of the brand among the entire audience. In other words, even those at whom the individual messages were not directly aimed could still respond to them in terms of an enhanced understanding of the BUPA brand and its proposition.

Communications launch

The plan was to lead with a series of individual television advertisements, each of which would communicate the most powerful and motivating benefits for some of the key services. These would be essentially fact-based commercials, conveying hard information which would enlighten and inform the relevant audience about a specific aspect of BUPA's offering.

These facts were to be, in effect, building blocks with which to construct a 'wall of communication' about BUPA. Specific facts about specific aspects of BUPA – namely BUPA hospitals, BUPA care homes, BUPA health assessment and provident status – would engage relevant consumers and prompt genuine interest and action. However, those facts would also in turn contribute to a broader appreciation of BUPA, not merely as a health insurer but as a wide-ranging, customer-oriented organization.

Criteria for success

Restoring awareness and increasing knowledge of BUPA's wider product offerings were thus the key criteria by which the new campaign was to be judged. The campaign would play a key role in motivating BUPA staff to deliver the brand promise.

Selecting appropriate media

The challenge was to say all that was needed to convince the audience that BUPA had something relevant for them. Television was clearly the most important medium, enabling communication about BUPA in the most personal and accessible way, to a wide range of audience segments. It would establish 'the personal health service' and generate the most effective 'halo' to build optimum response from other communication channels.

Campaign structure

The campaign comprised four television commercials, each featuring a scenario in which an individual receives a personally relevant message about one of the specific aspects of BUPA: self-pay operations, care services for the elderly, health screenings and provident status. Some additional activity complemented the TV campaign:

- Colour press advertising in national newspapers and magazines.
- BUPA Health Spots broadcast on Virgin FM.
- Direct marketing by each of the business units to convert awareness of individual services into sales leads.
- Sponsorship to provide media value and position BUPA as contributing to the nation's health.
- BUPA Great North Run televised on BBC1 and BBC2.
- BUPA Care Homes Open (world bowls) televised on BBC1 and BBC2.
- *Bodycheck* (a health and lifestyle magazine programme), supported by BUPA, televised on certain ITV stations.
- PR targeting national press, TV, radio and consumer magazines with news features on BUPA's unique range of services and advice on healthy living from BUPA doctors.

The response: external awareness

The key measure of the success of the new approach was that of brand awareness and communication. A new brand tracking study was commissioned from Millward Brown. Long-term trends on measures like spontaneous brand awareness and advertising awareness had been in decline and just before the new campaign was launched, the measures were at their lowest for five years.

The initial post-campaign measure showed immediate evidence of improvement, and this advanced as the campaign progressed. Consumer response to the campaign suggested that it was succeeding in generating interest in and prompting reappraisal of the brand. The process of repositioning had begun. By the end of 2000 the campaign had restored the brand and distanced it still further from its competitors.

- Spontaneous awareness had increased from 79 per cent to 89 per cent. That of BUPA's nearest competitor had fallen from 24 per cent to 20 per cent.
- Advertising recall went up from 32 per cent to 59 per cent, while competitor recall had fallen.
- Awareness of BUPA's services had increased and knowledge that BUPA offers services to all, not just to PMI members, was up from 23 per cent to 38 per cent.
- Key image dimensions also improved. For example, agreement that BUPA is growing more popular was up from 43 per cent to 54 per cent.
- Brand preference was the key dimension, and here BUPA's score increased from 52 per cent to 62 per cent, whilst the nearest competitor's fell from 32 per cent to 25 per cent.

Internal communication

A critical area of influence for the campaign was that of internal communications. From the outset it was intended to play an important role in building momentum behind the new positioning and direction for the brand, and foster a new understanding among staff. Internal communications involved working closely with each of the business units to improve customer focus. A series of roadshows was conducted to improve understanding of the value of marketing and the BUPA brand in the organization.

'The personal health service' became an effective encapsulation of the new positioning and strategy for the brand. The new approach was widely reported in the in-house newspaper, *BUPA Today*, where management were quoted endorsing the new campaign and its results.

In BUPA's annual survey of staff attitudes (SOP), the rating in terms of 'customer service mission' – the extent to which people working at BUPA feel the organization is customer-focused and acts to meet customer needs – increased from 61 per cent before the campaign to 66 per cent at the end. Anecdotal evidence also suggested that the new strategic and creative approach to the brand were enthusiastically received and highly influential internally.

Discussions with those with marketing responsibility in the various business units revealed that they had all adopted the new approach to positioning and communication and were actively seeking to fulfil it in the plans for their respective areas.

BUPA has also begun to work on a new set of brand guidelines to instil more branding discipline into all of its communications. The brand guidelines drive all manifestations of the brand. They apply to the tone of voice adopted by people in call centres when speaking to customers on the phone. They will equally apply to the signs outside BUPA hospitals. In short, the communication strategy should work in a very consistent way across the world.

The pay-out

The repositioning of BUPA has paid off in bottom-line terms, as well as in consumer awareness. The operating profit or surplus increased by 75 per cent between 1999 and 2000, from £46.7 million to £65.4 million. A distinctive positioning has been developed. Communication of that positioning has been put in place via a strategy that enables the full range of BUPA's services to be supported, both now and in the future. An integrated approach to communication has been achieved.

The specific objectives that were set have been met: higher awareness of both the brand and its services; broader appreciation of the role of BUPA and an enhancement of its image; a focus for internal understanding of, and confidence in, the new direction for the brand.

The catalyst for all this was the recognition of the need for and adoption of a new and comprehensive approach to the development of the brand, both internally and externally. BUPA's challenge is now to make the revolution permanent. That will require continually reinforcing the values that have proved powerful in effecting change, and constructive in winning customers, and enhancing competitiveness.

The editors comment

Repositioning an organization so well known for one specific activity – in BUPA's case health insurance – to achieve a much broader perception is not something that can successfully be achieved only through attention to the activities themselves and their promotion. Of course, BUPA did both of these things, but the organization also attended to the understanding and motivation of its managers and staff through innovative programmes and events. There is a truism that if people internally do not understand the vision and purpose, then there is very little chance of those vital principles being grasped externally. Moreover, in the delivery of service standards – vital in an industry like BUPA's where close customer contact is the core of the brand experience – the behaviour of staff is key to fulfilling the brand promise. If 'holistic' is a term that was first applied to medicine, then BUPA, most appropriately, has benefited from its application to its brand repositioning.

Chapter 8
A Team Approach: Manchester United

Peter Draper
Marketing Director, Manchester United plc

It was all very different in the beginning. The origins of Manchester United were modest, with simply the urge to play football prompting men at the carriage and wagon works of the Lancashire and Yorkshire Railway to form a team at their Newton Heath depot in 1878. Newton Heath played until they hit hard times in 1902 and were rescued from bankruptcy by the wealthy Manchester brewer, John H. Davies, who provided much-needed finance and promptly changed the name to Manchester United Football Club.

The new chairman soon led Manchester United into the club's first great era of success, and under Secretary/Manager Ernest Mangnall it won two Championships and then the FA (Football Association) Cup. Chairman Davies celebrated success by investing £60,000 in a new ground at Old Trafford. Yet good times were not guaranteed: in 1931 the club teetered on the edge of yet another bankruptcy and was nearly relegated. True to the spirit of Manchester United, however, the team fought back with real commitment. This was sorely tested when Old Trafford was blitzed in the Second World War, which meant a short stint playing at Maine Road (home of competing club Manchester City) until the ground was rebuilt in 1949.

This was to be the turning point of the club's fortune. It had not only a newly rebuilt stadium, but also a new manager, Matt Busby, who, returning home from the war, was about to wake the sleeping giant and eventually create the basis of the club you see today. By the mid-1950s the team had become a formidable force and, because of its youth, was known as the 'Busby Babes'. It was Busby, along with the club's directors, who made the decision to go against the Football League's wishes and introduce

Manchester United as the first English club to enter European competitions. The Munich air disaster on 6 February 1958, where eight key team players were killed, dealt the most savage blow imaginable, with the heart of the team destroyed in one tragic event.

However, the tragedy generated universal feeling for the club, and Busby set about rebuilding his team. He succeeded in assembling a squad of near-genius, including the formidable trio of George Best, Denis Law and Bobby Charlton. In 1968, ten years after the Munich disaster, Manchester United succeeded in becoming the first English club to win the European Cup. Sir Matt's reign saw the club winning five Championships, two FA Cups and the European Cup. Ever since this time, the club's popularity has been phenomenal. However, despite a succession of very capable managers, none could measure up to Sir Matt Busby's achievements until the arrival of Sir Alex Ferguson in 1986, which was the start of another new era. In 1990 the club won the FA Cup again. In 1991 it went on to win the European Cup Winners Cup. The accumulation of silverware continued with the 1992 Rumbelows Cup.

In line with the tradition of Manchester United firsts, the club became Champions of the newly-founded Premier League in 1992/3. Next season, the team went one better when it became one of the few this century to achieve the 'double' of the FA Premier League and the FA Cup. But more was to come: in 1996 it went into the history books as the only club ever to achieve the 'double' twice. More Premiership titles followed, with the club crowned champions in 1996/7, 1998/9, 1999/2000 and 2000/1. Arguably the most memorable year in the club's history was when it achieved the unique treble in 1999: the FA Cup, the Premiership and, most important of all, the much coveted Champions League Cup.

This history and aura of success are vital as the basis of the team's positioning in the sports world. Manchester United is first and foremost a team of outstanding excellence, with each individual player contributing to the overall talent that makes watching Manchester United so special. Throughout the club's illustrious history, it has produced teams of real quality. Old Trafford has always provided a unique and privileged platform for players' skills, and in return the players have provided the magic which has given Manchester United such universal appeal.

The club quickly established a tradition and culture that encouraged the individual to show his own unique flair and play with a freedom that has epitomized the club's style. Right from the early days at the turn of the century, Manchester United was associated with names that still stand out in the history of football. Matt Busby later put the accent on developing talent from within to create the Busby Babes. This was the team tragically torn apart at Munich; who knows what they might have gone on to achieve. The club was thus forced into the transfer market, but always with an eye for quality, with transfer records being repeatedly broken over the years. But the emphasis on home-grown youth returned under the management of Sir Alex Ferguson. The FA Youth Cup-winning class of 1992, which included now-famous players such as Ryan Giggs and Paul Scholes, is now a major contributor to the UK's most successful club.

Manchester United today

Manchester United is arguably the most famous football club in the world. Fans from Thailand to Zimbabwe and Argentina wear the strip and follow the team's performance. There are an estimated 10 million fans in the UK alone. While most of them never get to Old Trafford, they are nonetheless passionately devoted to the club, and therefore to the brand.

Manchester United was the first English team to win club football's most coveted prize, the European Cup, in 1968. Players such as George Best, Bobby Charlton and Denis Law in the 1960s and 1970s, Bryan Robson in the 1980s, Eric Cantona in the 1990s and David Beckham in the 2000s have worn that special red shirt. The most famous players could almost be considered as brands in their own right!

Club football, and particularly European club football, is now an industry worth billions of pounds, as demonstrated by the scale and importance of the biggest competition, the European Champions League. Qualification to this league is now a financial necessity for the big clubs, not only because it guarantees at least £15 million in revenue just for playing in stage one, but also because it helps the clubs to attract the world's best players.

Manchester United is unquestionably among the elite group of world-class football clubs, and arguably the only British club that can credibly claim to be so. Other members of this group would include Bayern Munich in Germany, Real Madrid and Barcelona from Spain, and Juventus, Lazio and Inter Milan from Italy. All these clubs play at large, modern stadiums with capacities of 70,000-plus; they can all afford to spend £25 million upwards on just one player; they all have fans around the world and, perhaps most importantly, they all regularly win honours.

Off the pitch, Manchester United has also grown as a business and it is now undisputedly the richest club on earth, with an annual turnover in 2000/1 of £130 million (source: Deloitte & Touche, December 2001). It is the successful diversification of the club's business concerns – always with football at the heart – which has led the club to this unique position.

Manchester United is therefore a successful brand, defined by any dimension. The history and culture are unique, and the club continues to build on this heritage. The 'product performance' is just about the best there is, which is essential to maintaining loyalty, interest and enthusiasm. Marketing strategies have been original and daring and have led to significant increases in revenues and profits. All of the basic building blocks for a world-class brand were in position.

But if all of these advantages were to be optimized, then development and management of Manchester United as a brand was essential. For football competes with other leisure pursuits for a share of free time, just as clubs compete with one another for cups and glory. Brand values must thus be honed and focused, and consistently expressed across all activities, to enable the brand promise to be delivered not just in competition results (which in Manchester United's case are likely to be superb, but are never inevitably so) but also through the whole range of brand experiences. And as the brand gains strength and credibility in areas off the field, as well as on it, so the opportunities for brand extension grow, and so does the need for effective brand management. The greater the growth, the greater the need for strategic development and control of the brand.

It was this need that led to a project, ongoing to this day, to first sharpen the communication of the brand, which was the area of greatest weakness and therefore greatest need.

The starting point

We decided at the outset to appoint brand consultants with a depth of experience in the field of sports branding. Together with one of their teams, we took on the task of analysing the communication of the Manchester United brand. On the basis of the analysis, we began an exercise to build the brand communications to the point where they not only represented Manchester United as we thought it should be, but also accommodated our long-term, wider global ambitions.

It was found that, over the years, decisions to do with the Manchester United brand and identity had been made piecemeal as issues arose and as individual activities were added on. So an array of different ways of visually expressing the brand had evolved. For example, each division within the organization had its own letterhead design, with its own version of the Manchester United name in various typefaces and with various emphases.

Which Manchester United would you like?
Confused visual branding prior to the exercise

Fans were also getting mixed messages. All over the world, they could tune in by satellite to matches, receive the *Manchester United Magazine*, buy team replicas, receive fixture lists, tickets and a variety of other printed material. And all over the world, they would see different versions of the marque, different graphic layouts and even different messages. An unkind neutral observer might have referred to this situation as 'brand identity anarchy'. As the club geared up to exploit more international marketing opportunities in association with similar 'big name' brands – such as Vodafone and Pepsi – and add media – such as the Internet – to the mix, the issue of brand management became increasingly pressing.

Even at the heart of the club, the Old Trafford stadium, there was little to see that expressed specific brand values or encouraged the pride, elation and excitement that fans must surely feel on approaching this football Mecca. Stadium identity graphics, direction signage, restaurant and retail graphics were all executed differently, diffusing the overall experience of the brand. Apart from anything else, the variety did not express professionalism, one of the club's core values. Taking into account all of this, and that Manchester United is extensively involved in licensing, it was critical to create a look and an identity that was unique, consistent and protectable.

The comprehensive visual audit of all the brand's diverse communications led us to a clear way forward. We had first to develop a single visual representation that would instantly call to mind the values and emotions associated with the brand. We then needed to create a system for applying this representation consistently and appropriately across every possible manifestation, from Beckham's jersey to the stadium identity to ticketing, from retail outlets to restaurant graphics. Our target audience was simply stated: *everyone who comes into contact with Manchester United*, from staff to journalists, from fans to sponsors, from national football organizations to local schools and so forth.

One simple, but significant change

The first, crucial stage of work was to establish hard and fast standards for the identity over and above the vagaries of fashion, creating a marque that would endure and retain its relevance for decades. This would, of course, be based upon the existing and very valuable brand properties. As the brand's success spread through merchandizing activities around the world, piracy had become a key issue. The new marque would have to be both unique and difficult to imitate.

The Manchester United crest was clearly the device most often associated with the club's communication. However, it not only appeared dated, but also existed in an amazing number of different versions on everything from numerous divisional letterheads to children's lunchboxes. The analysis of the key elements of the crest led us to one significant change concerning the communicative name of the club. To maximize the impact of the brand we were advised to remove the words 'Football Club'. We realized this was a potentially sensitive issue, given that football was our core activity. However, the consultants argued that the words 'Football Club' were simply redundant when applied to Manchester United, just like the word 'drink' is to Pepsi-Cola. Furthermore, it made even more sense when Manchester United's brand proposition was rapidly moving it from an English football club to an international leisure brand.

All the remaining elements were reworked, adding depth, richness and drama to what had been a rather flat image. The result is a far simpler, stronger, intensified brand statement – with the level of authority appropriate to an organization of Manchester United's international stature.

Before   After

New life and directness brought to the club crest, through simplification
and a three-dimensional treatment

A unique logotype for a unique brand

Many famous brands possess a unique logotype – Pepsi, Nike, Lego – and we felt that Manchester United should be no exception. Therefore the second part of the core identity development, together with the reworking of the crest, was the development of a unique, consistent logotype or way of writing Manchester United. And, as with the crest, we found that there were dozens of conflicting versions currently in use across the club's activities.

A customized, hand-drawn logotype was developed for use whenever Manchester United was required as a headline or prominent communication. From this was designed an entire one-off alphabet and a Manchester United visual vocabulary: a unique way of expressing the identity in print. This would enable the brand to achieve synergy between the many Manchester United properties, from Old Trafford to Alex Ferguson himself.

Before: different layouts, expressing different agendas

Keeping it consistent

Each of the divisions representing Manchester United's activities – such as catering or commercial or sponsorship – boasted its own individual stationery design. These had their own versions of the crest and used various typefaces and emphases. This situation had arisen naturally because each version of the Manchester United brand across each different medium had been created for a particular need at a particular time – and as such had its own individual merit. However, this kind of visual inconsistency added nothing to the building of the brand as a whole. For

After: consistency, expressing a common aim and an organized approach

example, the identity developed for Manchester United Radio was quite clever, but it communicated football radio rather than Manchester United radio. Again we needed to introduce a consistent approach. Our solution was the design of one strong, standard execution for Manchester United plc, which was then carried through to all the subsidiaries and divisions.

Having established the key identity elements, the brand team turned its attention to the next layer of communication, looking now to find a way of bringing some energy and excitement to the growing range of official

Manchester United consumer material, from coffee mugs to match tickets, from official merchandizing swing tags to museum tickets. The aim in each instance was to make every item a part of the Manchester United brand experience – something of value to keep.

We designed new red, crested match tickets, which now have a bank-note uniqueness, conveying a 'special occasion' feel beyond that obtained from a plain paper ticket. Helpfully, they also feature a 3D image of the stadium on the reverse, detailing turnstile numbers and stadium facilities. In such details is expressed an attitude of caring and concern towards fans who are, after all, the customers of the business.

Tickets: something of value to cherish as a memento of a special experience, an entrance to a brand world

The stadium and signage

The Old Trafford stadium itself is an important icon in the expression of the Manchester United brand. Mecca to the 10 million UK supporters alone, it has a distinctive shape and architectural presence. As part of the brand programme, we felt it important to find a simple, consistent way of representing it in every instance.

Old Trafford regularly attracts crowds of nearly 70,000 people and when you have this volume of fans converging on the stadium at the same time, clear wayfinding is paramount. Otherwise chaos can ensue and, even worse, the safety of fans could be compromised. Looked at another way, poor wayfinding can cause frustration and even alienation, which is the opposite of what we aim for.

Going to a match at Old Trafford is a highly charged, exciting experience for fans, but the audit of the wayfinding, graphics and signage around the stadium showed that they reflected none of the energy, importance or sense of occasion of a big game day. In some instances they were even ineffective in conveying key information. Using the stadium model which had been developed, a complete system of exterior signage was put together for Old Trafford. Each sign shows a different view of the stadium, giving an exaggerated perspective from the actual position. Banks of stands are colour-coded and correlated to ticket colours. A set of outer circle signs give general directional and facility information, guiding match-goers to the inner circle signs. These, in turn, detail more minutely the layout of that particular stand. Even the car park signs add something to the overall Manchester United presence. On the reverse of the distinctive red signs, a 3D location map shows all the major exit routes.

Merchandizing

Manchester United has a vast and growing licensing programme, part of a retail operation in which mail order plays a major role. The mail order catalogue goes out to an enormous international database each season, and is eagerly anticipated. The catalogue is an object which remains around in many thousands of homes for a long time and it really needed to express the club's values. So as part of the identity development, we gave it a complete overhaul. The result is not only a higher quality look, consistent with the new brand statement, but also cleaner, clearer and more contemporary.

Beyond just a football match

Once inside the Old Trafford stadium, fans can take advantage of two additional, secondary offers that are both part of the total brand experience: refreshment in the recently-launched Red Café, and the archive which is housed at the Museum and Tour Centre. We had plans to license the concept of the highly successful Red Café as far afield as Singapore. But if the café identity was to be relevant and recognizable anywhere outside the stadium, and thus exploit the value of the club's brand, we felt that it had to incorporate a direct reference to Manchester United.

The café's identity had only just been launched, and fortunately we were able to prefix it with the club name, transforming it into the 'Manchester

The Red Café: now the Manchester United Red Café, firmly linked to the club brand

United Red Café', and integrating the new logotype into the existing Red Café identity. The investment in this new sub-brand was thus not lost, but increased through the association with the main brand.

For the museum, we developed a new identity within the overall Manchester United look and then devised ways of applying this to all related material, from tickets to display units.

Fred the Red

Fans of any football club start young, and Manchester United boasts a huge following of junior supporters. Additionally, mascots are part of sport culture, so to appeal to the under-10 enthusiasts, the Club developed the 'Fred the Red' character. Loosely based on the figure from the club crest, Fred was a rather chubby cartoon devil who appeared on a wide variety of material, primarily aimed at this young audience.

We recognized that we had a really strong brand asset in Fred, and we were keen to exploit his licensing potential in children's products, including foods. With this in mind, we asked the branding consultants to take a look at him and his role within the brand experience, as well as his future potential. Apart from his rotund physique – hardly appropriate for a dynamic and fast-moving brand environment – Fred was apparently unclear about his role in relation to the team. On some occasions he featured as a caped, bow-tied player, sometimes in goal, sometimes not. At other times he was a supporter, casually clad in jeans and scarf. He needed a strategic makeover!

Eventually the new Fred emerged: a sleeker, more confident devil with a new sense of self-purpose as well as a new role in upholding brand values. Always a player, Fred now had a smart new strip and six standard poses. He now has his own logotype and a set of clear guidelines to be used to govern his use on products and in every other instance. Fred is now a valuable brand property in his own right and has been successfully marketed since his own relaunch.

Appealing to the under-10's, Fred the Red disports himself energetically over all sorts of merchandise and elsewhere

MU Finance

In October 2001 the club launched a new sub-brand, MU Finance, in partnership with established financial services providers such as the Bank of Scotland and Britannia Building Society. This aimed to exploit established brand trust in a new area of activity for the club, and the brand positioning was critical to its recognition and success. The approach adopted was to demystify the rather cold and complex language common to this sector and to associate the club with the customer's interests through prominent branding. Partners make a donation to the club for each product taken up by a United supporter. This is used to help develop the club both on and off the pitch.

MU Finance: a sturdy image for a product that needs to express strength and reliability

A new logotype was created, encompassing the crest within an authoritative holding device in the Manchester United colours. The written language and imagery on each leaflet expressed the brand values of warmth and accessibility for the target audience, but at the same time communicated the necessary authority and reassurance that are vital for the credibility of a serious financial services offer.

Our thoughts on brand identity

We believe that a successful brand identity is the sum of its parts, based on a unique positioning and brand values. The expression of the brand is via all of the contacts which target audiences have with it, and also through aspects such as the team's performance which, after all, is the basis for successful brand management of a football club. As with any other brand, the quality of the product is a prerequisite. This importance also extends to the history and culture of the club which, as we explained earlier, is unique. It would be easy to take these 'brand foundations' for granted, but without them there would be no Manchester United brand!

Those aspects of the brand that we can actively manage, in this case the visual elements, must then be sensitively and relevantly applied across all platforms. The range of potential applications hints at the size of the task:

- all stationery and presentation materials
- ticketing
- signage at the Old Trafford stadium
- all advertising applications
- the Red Café and Manchester United Museum
- merchandising stores around the world
- the team's kit
- the Club mascot, Fred the Red
- promotional material for potential sponsors
- 'on screen' usage, television in particular
- the *Manchester United Magazine* and match-day programmes
- the financial product
- all licensed material.

The emphasis therefore fell on the creation of a clear, flexible, visual branding system, with a comprehensive set of guidelines. This had two main objectives: first, to control the extension of the brand into markets beyond the north-west of England, and into a wide variety of sectors; and second, to engender vital internal cooperation and motivation behind the new branding so as to project a single, focused, powerful offer.

The results so far

From the start in mid-1997, it took about six months to complete the major phase of the project, and the new identity, in all its varying manifestations, began to roll out in early 1998. The public generally, and fans in particular, view Manchester United as a big and glamorous brand. This means everything it does comes under close scrutiny, particularly in its home city, and there was some predictably negative reaction to the dropping of the words 'football club'. Interestingly, this came mainly from tabloid newspapers, not from the fans.

Manchester United had been a famous and successful football club for many decades before this rebranding programme began. But this whole exercise served as a catalyst for many significant changes at the club, away from the pitch and first team, and away from the normal area of branding. For example, Manchester United had been previously organized into three separate businesses:

- The football club.
- Retail and merchandizing.
- Conferences and catering.

These units now became one, under the core brand, with a consistent identity and a much tighter supporting structure. The result was a fitter, clearer, more competitive organization.

The new branding also became the main cue and framework for corporate behaviour towards customers, be they fans, sponsors or shareholders. In this way, those within the club responsible for various areas of customer contact became aware of the impact – both negative and positive – of their actions. Regular fans and corporate guests enjoyed a much improved match-day experience, either functionally, such as finding the way to their seats, or emotionally, through a new crest and highly visible, unique branding.

Potential big brand sponsors such as Pepsi now saw a football club (a sector not renowned for sophisticated marketing techniques or expertise at the time) behaving in the same professional way that they themselves would adopt in communicating their brand. For example, the sponsorship side moved from being a tactical advertising sales operation to a clear professional package with a strategic rationale behind it. The core partners were 'Platinum Sponsors' led by Vodafone and Nike, but also including such names as Pepsi and Budweiser.

Fans could enjoy the 'Manchester United experience', be it a coffee in one of the Red Cafés, buying a Manchester United towel in one of the shops, or seeing an advertising poster in a consistent style from Salford in Manchester to Bangkok in Thailand. The club also started a regular fan satisfaction study run by a specialist customer relations company, which asked supporters for their views, positive and negative, on a range of issues from the price of a pint of beer and food quality, to atmosphere, safety and car parking arrangements. This is run annually, with a sample of around 2,000 match-going fans. The results are made available to all fans via a specific insert in the match day programme.

Fred the Red was now properly brought into the Manchester United fold, moving from an awkward mascot with an undefined role to a flexible character who communicated with younger fans in a visual language that appealed to them.

Staff were also much more highly motivated. There were no competing 'departments' and they all 'wore the same colours'. The telephone system, for instance, previously embraced about 80 separately-answered lines, causing great confusion to outside customers. A new, simpler exchange was introduced with one main, easy-to-remember number, creating more customer-friendly access.

The branding also added some real clarity and categorization to the diverse range of mail order items available, from simple items such as key rings to the ever-popular players' shirts.

The club now runs a very sophisticated and professional operation, but also sees itself as a pioneer with an urge to do something different. The major 13-year sponsorship with arguably the biggest brand in sport, Nike, is a case in point. This is no ordinary shirt deal. The length of the contract is a sign of mutual respect and confidence not just for the here and now, but also in a decade's time. Nike now have responsibility for all the club's merchandizing material from key rings to ketchups, sourcing product from around the club, branding it exclusively as Manchester United, distributing it and then handling all sales. No other English club enjoys such a sponsorship deal with such a famous brand with so wide a remit.

Old Trafford is now the largest stadium in British football and with over £150 million invested in it over the last ten years, its facilities are second to none. It was the host to the England versus Greece game in October 2001 and in the closing minutes it was a Manchester United player, David Beckham, who scored the goal that ensured England qualified for the 2002 World Cup.

In addition to winning many honours on the football field, the club is also a PLC and therefore under pressure to deliver results, from the City and from shareholders. We did not let them down. The club's turnover in 2001 was £129.6 million, an increase of 12 per cent over the previous year. The average attendance for all home games at Old Trafford was

67,100, the highest in European club football for 2000/1 and the reason for significant gate receipts of £46.2 million. Sponsorship turnover increased by 22 per cent to £22.5 million. Conference and catering revenues increased by 16 per cent to £7.8 million. Merchandizing revenues were equally impressive, bringing in £22.1 million.

From a public perspective, the worth and value of Manchester United had always been perceived as about 100 times greater than its actual market capitalization. 'This is largely because it is a brand with a rich heritage and an outstanding emotional appeal. We now have a complete new identity that strongly underpins all of this and encapsulates the unique values of the brand. It also adds stature and quality to the organization, fulfilling our wish to be right up there with the Mercedes-Benzes, Budweisers and Vodafones of this world,' says Peter Kenyon, now Chief Executive of Manchester United. With such a creative and professional redevelopment of all the club's brand communications, it is now well placed to grow. As Peter Kenyon adds, 'We now have a unique and consistent platform that can continue to move the brand successfully forward in years to come.'

The editors comment

The concept of a football club as a brand is a recent one, and therefore this case must be seen in the light of this. The discipline of brand management has enabled the club to identify and exploit an element of brand value as a strategic success factor in its long-term success. Brand management so far has been seen mainly in marketing and design terms, but it has certainly impacted on corporate strategy. It is obvious that the team's performance is a principal driver of the club's reputation, and therefore a dimension of a holistic brand, although not consciously within the brand remit. The concepts and implementation of strict brand design guidelines across all manifestations help the club to deliver on its brand promise over a broad spectrum of branded experiences. As Peter Draper says, 'everything [Manchester United] does comes under close scrutiny'. The implications for the brand are clear: the consistency and performance of all dimensions keeps the brand at the forefront.

Chapter 9
A Brand Without Limits: Virgin

Will Whitehorn
Director of Corporate Affairs, Virgin Group Ltd

> I believe there is almost no limit to what a brand can do, but only if used properly.
>
> **Sir Richard Branson**

Introduction

Just what is Virgin? A high street entertainment retailer? An airline? A passenger train operator? A mortgage provider? A credit card provider? A mobile telephone company? A car retailer? A swimwear and lingerie retailer? The world's third largest health and leisure operator? Virgin is all and none of these – and many more besides!

Virgin is an example of a brand that has true holistic credentials. Its brand promise is strongly understood and interpreted by its customers as 'being for them'. It has evolved into one of the most resilient and flexible brands in the UK, if not the world. Yet the Virgin brand has not developed from conventional business models. Its history is of entrepreneurial risk-taking, grasping opportunities that arose, partnering with like-minded individuals or companies who could provide specific expertise and a built-in mission to challenge the norm.

The brand and corporate culture are indivisible. The brand attributes shape all company transactions and interface with internal and external audiences. There has been a consistency of corporate vision which, unlike most corporate models, does not reside in growing an expertise and position in one sector. Consistency has come from an attitude towards doing business which is philosophical as well as commercial.

Over the years, Virgin has grown from a music business – retailing and recording popular music – into a venture capital business that invests in Virgin branded businesses with strategic business partners. The power of the Virgin name has both fuelled its original expansion and enabled it to establish successful businesses in a number of non-related areas. It is the Virgin brand promise and the culture of the Virgin organization that unites these businesses.

Today Virgin is the third most recognized brand in Britain, and has considerable recognition around the world. Yet the man behind its success, Sir Richard Branson, claims no master plan or business practice – just a belief that the Virgin name, and what it has come to stand for, can be applied to many different products and services, and that his vision of his entrepreneurially-based company could be the platform for a successful and wide-ranging business.

In this chapter we will look at how a small number of key guiding principles have enabled Virgin to become one of the world's pre-eminent brands, one that lives its vision throughout the organization and in its relationships with its customers. We will examine the relationship between the brand and its founder, Richard Branson, and how this has contributed to the brand personality. Maintaining the consistency and integrity of the brand is a key focus for management, and we outline the measures taken to manage this. Finally, the chapter concludes with a view of where Virgin is going in the future.

Sir Richard Branson, Virgin's intrepid and legendary founder

The development of the brand and evolution from a music business to a multi-faceted global empire

My vision for Virgin has never been rigid and changes constantly, like the company itself.

Richard Branson

Virgin is unique. It was the brainchild of Richard Branson who, by the age of 18, had the vision and foresight to realize it was possible to create a brand that could be applied to many different products. Starting a magazine for young people, *Student*, he already had the idea that the concept could cover many other products and services for young people: a student travel service, perhaps a bank.

So the mindset right from the beginning was one of eclectic ambition. There were to be no limits to the thinking about the direction the company could move in. When the first Virgin business started in 1970, the venture was a mail order music business. (In fact it was very nearly named 'Slipped Disc Records', to match the irreverent mood of the times. This brand might have found it more difficult to achieve the 'stretch' to financial products, aircraft and mobile phones.)

Although other businesses were developed and some went by the wayside, music recording, publishing and retailing were the main focus of Virgin for the first 14 years of its existence. Virgin Music grew to be one of the top three independent record labels in the UK, with extensive businesses around the world. From its early days, Virgin Music constantly reinvented itself to stay with the latest trends in music, and always achieved a 'cool' position in the market place. Thus Virgin's music heritage brings it a liaison with the glamorous world of popular music, which has enabled the brand to retain its appeal to the youth market, while its first customers were ageing.

Many of the early businesses were associated with music, although by 1983 the company had recognized and involved itself with the trend for computer games and launched Virgin Interactive. However, 1984 brought the most radical departure for Virgin with the launch of Virgin Atlantic Airways. This was Richard Branson at his most entrepreneurial.

131

The current livery of Virgin Atlantic is the confident statement of a mature airline

He recognized an industry which was dominated by a small number of large players, British Airways dominating British commercial aviation. Above all he recognized that most of the competitors still had an engineering mindset: passengers were just cargo to be moved from A to B.

Branson examined his own experience of international jet travel: the discomfort, boredom and dullness of the flights. He determined that Virgin could not only do it better, it could do it differently. The major breakthroughs in airline safety and performance had been made: to arrive safely and reasonably on time were now customer expectations. So his vision was of an airline where passengers would enjoy their time in the air, with better entertainment, and friendly, well-trained staff. Business passengers would be given the luxury of first class treatment, at club class prices. The history of Virgin Atlantic has been to launch new improvements that other airlines have to match: in-flight massage, arrivals lounges and a new class, Premium Economy. From Virgin Atlantic, the company developed a holiday business, invested in a short-haul continental airline based in Brussels, Virgin Express, and in 2000 launched Virgin Blue in Australia, a low-cost carrier flying 16 routes.

The 1990s were a period of considerable change for the Virgin Group. In 1992 Virgin Music was sold to EMI for $1 billion; four years later another record label and publishing company, V2, was launched to leverage the expertise in the company's management team. Music has been a powerful generator of positive brand attributes for Virgin around the world: the return to the music industry ensures the brand stays in touch with young people and retains its 'cool' credentials.

The V2 logotype

A further interest in travel came in 1997/8 when Virgin won two licences to operate passenger rail services in Britain. On the face of it, Virgin's decision to bid for (and win) franchises for two parts of Britain's beleaguered national rail network were ambitious to the point of corporate lunacy. Britain's railway infrastructure had been under-funded for decades and passengers, dismayed by delays, high prices, a horrible travel experience and poor service had, where they could, deserted the railway for their cars. Those locked into the use of trains such as urban commuters were demoralized and angry.

The Conservative government had decided that privatization was the key, and accordingly sold off the tracks and maintenance to Railtrack and key franchises to a number of key operators. This meant that the train operators were at the mercy of Railtrack with its heritage of chronic under-investment leading to the poor state of the railway network. This was evidenced most dramatically in 2000, when a major accident resulted in virtually six months of chaos and delays as tracks were checked and repaired.

It was precisely the kind of challenge that appealed to Sir Richard Branson: the opportunity to put the consumer first, improve standards to Virgin criteria and provide a fun travel experience. A less confident management may have doubted the wisdom of attaching the Virgin brand

to such a risky enterprise. However, the British government was obviously aware of the power of the name as its use was a condition of a successful bid.

Virgin Rail has had a steep learning curve as the extent of the lack of investment on the infrastructure became apparent, leading to cancellations and delays. Along with other franchise operators, Virgin has struggled to deliver the service it promised, and delays in track

New rolling stock for Virgin Trains: these trains are coming into service, displacing the old ones inherited from British Rail, satisfying pent-up customer demand for improved comfort and facilities upgrades have put back the introduction of new, improved rolling stock. However, by 2003 this should be in place, and Virgin will have the most modern railway carriages in Europe on its services.

Rail is undoubtedly a high profile part of Virgin's business, but research conducted by the company indicates that the brand image has been resilient enough to withstand the criticism from customers and media. Virgin is credited with taking on board a run-down and outdated service and 'having a go' to create something better. When the 'Virgin experience' is finally successfully delivered, Virgin Rail will be a further opportunity to consolidate the brand's reputation with customers.

Retail has been a consistent part of the business since the early days, with the offering now consolidated into Megastores and V2 retail stores. Embracing the Internet, retailing of cars, bikes and wines was added to financial services and travel products via Virgin.com.

A venture capital specialist who recognized the sector as a ripe target for the company put the idea for financial services to Virgin. It was a classic Virgin launch: a simple index-linked product which was easy to understand and easily explained and which cut out the broker who traditionally had taken a large commission. Virgin created a joint venture with an experienced partner, initially Norwich Union, and later AMP. Richard Branson commented, 'Virgin Direct may appear to be an incongruous departure for Virgin, the rock and roll company: it was a lateral leap in the same way as it had been from records to airline. But it is still all about service, value for money and offering a simple product.'

A Virgin Megastore

The Virgin Mobile logotype: part of the family, but distinctly different

Virgin's latest ventures have taken it into the field of mobile telephony, via a joint venture with One2One in the UK, SingTel in Asia and Cable & Wireless in Australia. The opportunity for selling fixed telephony has been generated by the joint venture with London Electricity to provide utilities through Virgin Energy. With a programme of acquisition in the UK and South Africa, Virgin Active health clubs have made Virgin the third largest health and leisure operator in the UK.

The Virgin business and strategic vision

Virgin's business interests are now primarily in travel and leisure; holidays; cars; finance; soft drinks; wines; cosmetics and publishing. There are 210 companies worldwide, employing over 31,000 people. Total revenues in 2000 exceeded £3.9 billion. At the beginning of the twenty-first century the Virgin business looks very different from its humble beginnings. A simple strategic vision has emerged of a much more diverse group. Non-Virgin branded businesses are gradually being divested. Some operations, such as the computer games business, Virgin Interactive, have been sold but continue to operate the Virgin name under licence.

In 1990 the group turnover was split between Retail, Air Travel and Music and Media, with the latter accounting for 46 per cent of turnover; by the year 2000, although 90 per cent of turnover was still from three sectors, one of them, Rail, was new and already accounted for 16 per cent. The sale of Virgin Music and many media-related businesses had fuelled growth in other sectors and reduced the company's reliance on this business.

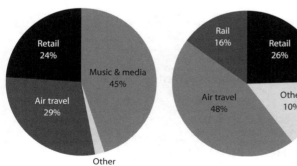

Other

Mobile 2%

Internet(.com) 2%

Drinks 2%

Financial services 2%

Music & media 1%

Hotels & leisure 1%

Virgin Group turnover 1990   Virgin Group turnover 2000

After only one year of operation, Virgin Mobiles accounted for 2 per cent of turnover, with connections in the UK exceeding 1.3 million. Joint venture companies in Asia and Australia were under way, and Virgin plans further expansion into the United States, Europe, South Africa and Canada. Air travel dominates, but now comprises three businesses: Virgin Atlantic, Virgin Express and Virgin Blue.

The Virgin vision

First and foremost, any business proposal has to sound fun. If there is a market that is just served by two giant corporations, it appears to me that there's room for some healthy competition. As well as having fun, I love stirring the pot. I love giving big companies a run for their money, especially if they're offering expensive, poor-quality products.

Richard Branson

Virgin is a 'branded venture capitalist', aiming to leverage the strengths of the Virgin brand in situations where the company can deliver significant market impact and enhance shareholder value. The brand's key values are:

- quality
- value for money
- innovation
- fun
- competitive challenge.

Guidelines for new business ventures state that they must be in areas that:

- are consumer focused and under-served
- can deliver 30 per cent compound growth per year in shareholder value
- can support a global or multi-regional roll-out
- can reach significant scale within three years
- are synergistic with existing Virgin businesses
- can provide an appropriate realization of value for shareholders within three to five years (IPO, trade sales).

The focus on businesses that are consumer driven is the common thread that can be seen in all Virgin businesses. Virgin Cola was launched to challenge the duopoly of Pepsi and Coke, British rail passengers had been experiencing poor service for years, and banking and personal finance had seen little championing of the consumer from the big banks.

Virgin Group Investments Limited is the powerhouse of Virgin, led by Sir Richard Branson, who is supported by a management team who have an eclectic range of individual skills and competencies, ranging from accountancy to marketing. To improve focus on core areas of competence, the Virgin Group has been given a new management structure.

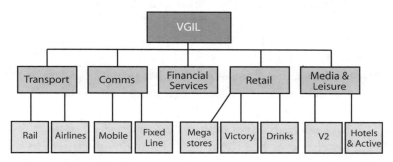

Virgin Group management structure

The Virgin business of the twenty-first century has been put on firm foundations in recent years, with this streamlined management which can move quickly to identify new opportunities or advise on problems within the businesses. However, the Virgin branded companies are all run as independent businesses, with a member of the VGIL management team sitting on their board. This ensures:

- The companies are ring-fenced and trade independently of other Virgin businesses.
- The VGIL member brings the knowledge of the corporate culture and best practice from other businesses, and the ability to manage the consistency of the brand across different sectors.
- The companies are able to develop their businesses and use their own flair and expertise to create growth and profitability.

- The businesses benefit from association with the Virgin heritage, and this in turn is protected from a maverick company acting in a way that lowers the brand reputation.

What Virgin brings to these enterprises is the brand, management and some investment. These are valuable propositions which have attracted major players such as Royal Bank of Scotland and AMP in the financial arena, London Electricity and Singapore Airlines in the travel sector.

The development of the logo and brand image

'You've got the X factor, the Y factor – you've got every factor there is,' says Gerry Pencer, the chief executive of Cott Corporation. 'People like Virgin, they trust the name; they'll buy a product because it's a Virgin product.'

The most influential interface between customers and the brand is through the 170 Megastores and 100 V2 shops around the UK and across the world. Through high street exposure and high store traffic, the Virgin experience reaches out directly to tens of millions of customers a week. Virgin undertook research through HPI in 2000 which placed Virgin as the most admired company in the UK behind Marks and Spencer and Boots. Among men it was the most admired company. This unprompted awareness demonstrates the power of retailing to create a bond between customers and company.

Virgin Net has 600,000 ISP customers (making it the number three ISP in the UK) and 700,000 entertainment users. Virgin.com is an ISP and content provider with 18,000 pages online, receiving 1 million visitors a week. Henley Centre (UK) research revealed Virgin is in the top three most trusted online brands. Trainline is now the number one UK travel site by bookings, and Virgin Atlantic/Holidays is in the top five sites for visits. During 2001, 50 million UK customers visited these sites.

The Virgin logo
Back in 1970 the Virgin name was chosen as it was catchy, slightly risqué (in fact it took three years before the Patent Office would register it) and

was matched with a logo of a naked lady back to back, designed by Roger Dean, a famous illustrator of record sleeves. Early in the 1970s a new design was called for, and it is the stuff of urban legend that graphic designer Trevor Key had been doodling designs for the brand name. He threw one on the floor and it was selected by Richard Branson, and with modification is the one which has been used ever since.

The use of a handwriting graphic brings personality and the personal touch to the mark, as well as a feeling of energy and action. Like another famous brand, McDonald's, the Virgin logo lends itself to adaptation: the exaggerated 'V' is synonymous with the brand and has enabled other brands such as V2 to be developed from it. It has proved itself flexible enough to stretch across the tail fin of a jumbo jet, a can of cola, a shop fascia, and to adorn a credit card. The colour red is a powerful memory-trigger and Virgin guards its use jealously. It provides another element of consistency in the branding wherever it touches the consumer, whether it be promotional material, the red Virgin Cola can or the seats in Virgin trains and planes.

Protecting the integrity of the brand

Today the brand itself is legally owned by one company, Virgin Enterprises Limited, which is responsible for over 1,500 trademark registrations, all in 200 countries. The brand's visual integrity is guarded by the Brand Book which explains the guidelines in using the logo. Infringements that have crept in over the years are now being eradicated. In particular, the use of descriptions added to the logo in the 'Virgin' typeface is actively discouraged to protect the integrity of the trademark.

As all trademark registration is done corporately, this gives some measure of control over variations in the use of the logo, development of the names of Virgin products and services, and any special requests for different colours. The company tries to accommodate requests where possible if it will help to promote the brand.

The word Virgin itself is strongly protected within the company, avoiding the use of obvious puns and creating words out of the virgin name such as 'virgininformation' as these are difficult to register and/or dilute the trademark protection.

On the Net, Virgin prefers its associate companies to route customers through the Virgin.com homepage:

- It negates the need for people to search if there is just one web address.
- A single web address gives consistency to all advertising, promotional and other material.
- It strengthens the virgin.com site as THE place to go for information on Virgin.

For those wishing to have their own URL, it is possible for a branch name to be created from the Virgin.com site. Creating new domain sites is allowed by Virgin but not encouraged. All registrations are undertaken by Virgin Enterprises Limited, which has already registered 2,000 domain names that incorporate 'virgin' in some way. Almost all of these are protective measures to stop other people from using them.

All Virgin advertising is booked through one media buying agency who have many years' experience of working with the company. This ensures that conflicts do not occur and that any advertising using logos incorrectly or not in the spirit of the Virgin brand has a further opportunity to be picked up. Regular meetings are held with the PR, marketing and quality assurance staff of the various companies to share best practice and ensure alignment with common goals. When one of the businesses has a particular strength, then executives from that business are invited to share their learnings at the functional team meetings. Individuals are also seconded to other parts of the business: for example, an employee at Virgin Mobile in the UK has recently undertaken to make presentations on customer service to the Virgin Mobile companies in Australia and Asia. It is also one of the responsibilities of the VGIL board member who sits on individual company boards to monitor business practice and promotional activities to ensure alignment with the brand guidelines.

Growing and protecting the reputation
Public relations has always been at the forefront of Virgin marketing activity, for managing the reputation of the brand through the media, aggressively

searching for positive coverage and defending negative publicity. Public relations is a board level position at Virgin, unlike many British corporations. Every day Branson and senior managers check press cuttings and staff letters as a priority to take the temperature of the brand's health. The company actively challenges incorrect statements, issues regular information about its products, and lobbies for changes in regulations that harm the business or are against the consumer interest.

Grabbing media headlines has developed into a skill at Virgin, using numerous humorous stunts featuring Richard Branson to launch new products. The value of coverage for Richard Branson's boat and balloon record attempts was measured in millions of pounds and was instrumental in building global brand awareness in the 1990s.

The role of Sir Richard Branson: the brand champion

The success of Virgin is inseparable from its high profile chairman and founder. Through his championing of his companies, cheeky PR stunts and intrepid ballooning adventures, Richard Branson has become one of the best-known businessmen in the world. He has won a reputation, particularly in Britain, that is unique among business leaders: celebrity, daredevil sports personality and business visionary. His business affairs are not just for the financial pages, but of interest to the general public. His image is of David taking on Goliath, as he has challenged British Airways, the traditional banking sector and the 'big two' mobile telephone companies, to name just three.

Despite the difficulties that have beset Virgin since taking on two rail franchises, research shows that Sir Richard's own personal reputation has in fact been enhanced among the general public. They feel that he is 'having a go' to make a difference, and despite the media's many attempts to highlight the problems with the service, both Sir Richard and the Virgin brand have not been damaged.

There are guidelines for Sir Richard's involvement in the businesses, and the general rule is that the managing directors should be the spokespersons and figureheads. In fact the golden rule, is, if possible, don't use him! Because

Percentage of people who believe that certain words apply to the Virgin brand/Richard Branson

	Virgin	*Richard Branson*
Popular	60	58
Ambitious	50	74
Friendly	49	50
Professional	48	51
Going places	45	43
Trustworthy	39	35
Trendy	39	24
Independent	38	41
Clever	35	56
Different	35	34
Fun	34	35
Determined	34	67
Down-to-earth	34	40
Innovative	27	34
Daring	23	38
Bit of a rebel	18	31
Unique	17	23
Unconventional	14	24
Kind	12	10
Traditional	5	7
Inconsistent	2	3
Unreliable	2	2

he has such a high profile, his exposure is carefully managed to ensure that he is used strategically and that there is not overkill. He is usually featured in the PR launch of new businesses, after which their managements become the new face of the business and own the communications.

Virgin Atlantic, Virgin Money and Virgin Trains are the businesses most likely to involve Sir Richard because of their high profile and complexity. He is a frequent commentator on regulatory issues, and has the unique ability to span multi-national governmental concerns such as airline monopolies and still be a relevant commentator for young people on mobile telephony. Research into people's attitude to the Virgin name and its founder showed that in many cases they were very similar, and the profile of the chairman is undoubtedly supportive to the brand.

Living the brand within Virgin

> We embarked on consciously building Virgin into a brand which stood for quality, value, fun and a sense of challenge. We also developed these ideas in the belief that our first priority should be the people who work for the companies, then the customers, then the shareholders. Because if the staff are motivated then the customers will be happy, and the shareholders will then benefit through the company's success.
>
> **Richard Branson**, *Money Programme* Lecture 1998

Virgin works hard to retain its culture, ensuring that staff understand the vision and need for customer focus. The same thread of challenge, irreverence, care for consumers and fun run through all its businesses, and this is also maintained throughout internal communications. Everyone in the company is a member of a 'tribe' and receives a monthly newsletter from the centre which offers discounts on all the Virgin products, plus specially negotiated deals from other suppliers. The company has its own Intranet known as the ExtraNet which is an excellent source of information on the companies' activities, and various presentations can be downloaded.

Virgin has a 'celebration culture': teams are expected to reward their staff for good performance, and there is rarely a week goes by without at least one party!

Each new business that is started under the Virgin brand name is now given a thorough induction into the Virgin culture via videos and meetings. Virgin's customer care standards are critical to the business, and so each business needs to understand this. A new business may wish to operate to standards common to its sector, and needs to be encouraged through its VGIL board member and the corporate Standards and Assurance team to stretch its service performance targets higher.

Because Virgin is a big brand made up of lots of small companies, every time a venture gets too big it is divided up into smaller units. This provides employees with greater incentives to work and to perform. Training is given a strong emphasis, again sharing best practice within the companies, and follows a McKinsey model encompassing empowerment, monitoring, motivation, communication and strategy.

Employees are encouraged to 'bring their personality to work', and interface with customers is based on the original guiding principles developed by Richard Branson for Virgin Atlantic. Customer service is built around the belief that 98 per cent of complaints come from people who do not just want to screw the system. Virgin believes that the first person to know about a complaint is the best person to deal with it. So staff are empowered to solve problems, rather than pass the buck.

Because of the very nature of the Virgin brand, many complaints go direct to Richard Branson, which is the best way of management knowing how healthy its customer service is. The company also welcome comments, ideas and suggestions from staff, the company credo being that no one has a monopoly on a good idea. And Richard Branson leads from the front by continually staying in touch with customers, particularly in the air and rail businesses, and passing on suggestions and ideas to managers. The business constantly strives to surprise and delight customers – and keep the 'wow' factor with good service, going beyond the expected.

The future for Virgin

As far as I'm concerned the company will never stand still. It has always been a mutable, indefinable thing....

Richard Branson

The Virgin brand is now highly regarded in Europe and around the world. It has developed core businesses in the fields of travel, leisure, music, entertainment and leisure retailing, financial services and mobile telephony. The company plans to build a number of truly global businesses from a strong consumer base in the UK. Virgin Atlantic has already established a presence in most of the world's major economies and is comfortably and profitably providing service to the world's business community and independent travellers. Key targets for a global presence are travel, mobile telecommunications, entertainment retailing and music.

Where considerable growth will come, particularly in the UK, is by exploiting the opportunities for 'convergence marketing' that are emerging from the concurrent convergence of e-commerce and mobile telephony technologies. It is envisaged that these opportunities will provide significant consumer benefits, while at the same time enhancing shareholder value.

The policy of active venture capital over the next decade through growing branded businesses and taking them public will realize value for the shareholders. Travel (both rail and air), financial services and content businesses will be particular beneficiaries of these developments, with more efficient yield management and lower transaction costs. A single branded retail chain, split between large Megastores and smaller V shops, will be the second part of Virgin's 'clicks and mortar' strategy developing from e-commerce and mobile telecommunications.

Cross-selling and promoting of the different products and services can only accelerate, and give more and more consumers the chance to sample the Virgin experience. Consumers today can rely on Virgin for their holiday, rail travel, favourite CD, mobile phone, credit card and pension, work out at a Virgin health club and relax afterwards with a glass of wine provided by Virgin Wines, reading a Virgin published book by an electric light fuelled by Virgin Energy.

By its diversification, Virgin has many opportunities to create a good reputation with customers, and dilute the effects of a bad experience with one of its products or services. It has a strong heritage to build upon, which will need nurturing. Projects like Virgin Rail will not be given the benefit of the doubt for ever, but a successful outcome will prove even more conclusively that the Virgin business ethic meets the needs of the consumer and is one of the most powerful brands in the market place.

Never a brand to fight shy of a challenge, the company's aim is to place Virgin among the top 20 global brands by 2010. We believe we will do this by maintaining the brand standards and corporate ethos which is so firmly entrenched in this company at all levels and which guides all our communications.

The editors comment

Virgin is a prime example of a brand-led company. Everything Virgin does is conceived and determined by the 'ability' of the brand to support the launch and development of a range of seemingly disparate ventures. But, as Will Whitehorn points out, this holistic brand is indivisible from the culture and the day-to-day running of Virgin companies, and their contacts with millions of customers in a varied range of circumstances. The fact that, in this case, the guiding vision is that of one man – Sir Richard Branson – does not lessen the achievement, nor should it distract from the proven truth that companies with strong visions are generally the most successful. It can surprise few that Virgin stands for 'quality, value, fun and a sense of challenge', since these attributes run through all of its business activities, from selection of which to be in, to promotion and Branson's own activities. If anyone lives the brand, Branson certainly does!

Chapter 10
A Professional Image: CMS

Richard Taylor
Chairman, CMS

The marketing of professional services is not a new subject, but it has lagged far behind marketing in other business areas, for several reasons. First, professions were for generations bound by their own rules of promotion, or rather non-promotion, which made them unable to advertise and discouraged direct approaches to prospective clients. The understanding of a 'client' as a customer in the normal business sense was not encouraged, and the discreet term 'business development' – mostly carried out through networking with business and social contacts – was the nearest that auditors and solicitors (along with engineers and architects) got to marketing or selling.

When those attitudes began to change in the 1960s and 1970s, there were attempts to reach markets by more direct means. PR was certainly used to effect, and minor ways to circumvent the professional ban on advertising were explored, such as corporate advertising masquerading as advertising for personnel. It was not until professional rules were relaxed, however, that things really began to change.

By the 1990s, Anglo-Saxon law firms were well versed in marketing techniques, the larger ones having set up in-house departments staffed by professionals, and they were creating a significant output across the promotional spectrum. Whether their purpose and efforts were fully understood or appreciated by all partners is questionable, but they were accepted as necessary to the business process. In Germany, more conservative business thinking ensured that traditional notions of professionalism continued to be held more strongly, although some firms did employ marketing personnel. Larger forces, however, were about to influence the situation.

Globalization – or at least internationalization and consolidation – were, and are, the principal forces for change. Accountancy firms experienced this some time before law firms, resulting in what became known as the 'Big Eight' firms (later, through consolidation, the 'Big Five', and now going through a period of readjustment). These mega-firms were often associations of individual national partnerships that agreed to conform to certain standards, including those of external presentation. Law firms grew in size, too, and many London-based firms had substantial overseas networks, but it was not until pressure for pan-European legal services increased, resulting in cross-border associations, amalgamations and mergers, that serious consideration began to be given to global 'branding'.

The founding of CMS

CMS Cameron McKenna, one of the top ten UK law firms, was itself the product of a merger and was close to completing a process of integration when CMS was founded. CMS (a set of initials deriving from 'Cameron McKenna' and 'Sigle', one of the constituent founders of Hasche Sigle Eschenlohr Pelzer and of CMS in Germany) was intended initially as a European association of law firms, brought together to offer comprehensive, pan-European services to clients. It was founded in 1998, and by 1999 consisted of firms in the UK, Germany, Austria, the Netherlands, Belgium and Switzerland. Practical steps were taken to establish it, perhaps the most important being the Practice Area Groups which were (and are) composed of representatives of the various specializations from all of the constituent firms. The creation of CMS was a far-sighted move to respond to client needs and market opportunities, to build a pan-European (later a global) firm in cooperation with like-minded firms in various countries. Full integration, in the long term, was always intended, but the process was seen as evolutionary rather than revolutionary.

After some two years it became evident that both internal

TRANSNATIONAL LEGAL SERVICES

The original CMS logotype: some saw it as the globe, some as brackets. Either way, its acceptance was low

and external acceptance of CMS as an integrated, pan-European entity were too low. One of the most obvious manifestations of the problem was that two entirely different corporate design systems were in use, one in the UK and the other in continental Europe. This resulted partly from the relatively recent merger between Cameron Markby Hewitt and McKenna's which had formed Cameron McKenna. At that time, a new visual identity had been produced, which had been successful in providing visual unity, as well as a somewhat 'different' face to the market. Having united under this new 'flag', Cameron McKenna were understandably reluctant to give it up to conform to the rest of CMS.

Research into CMS identity

The low acceptance and profile of CMS, plus the glaring inconsistencies in presentation, led us to employ the services of a consultancy (but a different one this time) to sort out a situation fraught with preconceptions, territorial pride and cultural diversity. The German dimension, the German firm being the largest after Cameron McKenna itself, was of great importance and sensitivity, particularly with respect to their conservative attitude towards 'branding', so a consultancy with proven experience in the German market was selected.

Cameron McKenna itself was the only CMS firm with a substantial and dedicated marketing department, so the project was largely run from London, where the consultants were also based. In the light of this, and the size of Cameron McKenna in relation to the other firms (over 1,500 people in comparison to 700 people at Hasche Sigle Eschenlohr Pelzer), it was imperative to avoid the impression that this was in any way a UK-centric project, which was successfully achieved, as will be explained.

After carrying out desk research – Cameron McKenna had a considerable body of material about the market, its own position and that of the other firms – the consultants carried out a series of in-depth, one-to-one interviews with partners and others in all the individual firms at their own offices. These, of course, confirmed some of the things which we already knew, but the strength of feeling was noticeable, and all findings had to be viewed in the light of the fact that those interviewed, as with all partners in professional firms, are normally focused intently on fee-earning work. They naturally feel that non-client tasks distract them from their professional work, and therefore directly affect the bottom line. The degree of interest in this project, and the willingness to devote time to it, were therefore all the more remarkable.

A wide range of views was expressed, but it was possible to draw clear conclusions, among which were:

- Given the slow progress to date, there was some scepticism about the overall commitment to CMS.
- No distinctive CMS culture had yet formed, which was not surprising as no target culture had been defined.
- The name 'CMS' had been accepted well in some areas, but not all.
- Cameron McKenna partners were eager not to lose the goodwill associated with a strong corporate design that they had invested in over a three year period.
- The difference in visual styles was seen as contradictory to the whole idea of CMS, and potentially very damaging.
- Few people had thought through the issue of differentiation from the competition, except the 'federal' concept which was different from the full mergers pursued by some.
- Results were demanded – quickly.
- Most emphatically, people wanted to see substance behind the CMS brand, starting with a basic internal understanding of its nature and aims, and carried through to its influence on day-to-day activities.

A number of external interviews was also carried out, which confirmed a rather 'shadowy' awareness and understanding of CMS.

Developing a shared concept

The results of all the interviews, together with the consultants' ideas on competitive market positioning and the naming structure, were presented to a meeting of the firm's Executive Committee in the Hasche Sigle Eschenlohr Pelzer office in Hamburg. The occasion proved to be a milestone. Because views were so openly presented and discussed, issues were faced and accepted in a very constructive atmosphere, and any lingering suspicions of branding being superficial, or a waste of executive time, evaporated for good.

A draft vision, mission and values statement was one of the things presented at the meeting, as the basis for our own understanding of ourselves and as the first step towards giving substance to the brand. We were aware that such statements are often near-useless generalizations which bear little relationship to real, day-to-day activities, but our consultants suggested a process to confirm or challenge these draft values, which would in itself act as a catalyst towards a distinctive culture for CMS, as well as recommending subsequent steps for communication and for realizing the values.

In the workshop that introduced this process, doubts were again dispelled as we collaboratively fought towards our shared concept of CMS and its core values. In a multi-national group, this is far from straightforward. Our moderator was, rightly, determined that, as a prerequisite to formulating any statement, we should have a firm baseline of understanding. This involved questioning many seemingly ordinary words to ensure we had a common meaning. Of course, we worked in English – the nearest thing we have to a universal business language – and it was amazing to discover that even simple words had nuances, either for we Brits or for our continental colleagues, which had completely escaped us and which could have caused serious problems in any statement of corporate purpose, had we not been forced to find better alternatives.

This aspect of international communications is a difficult one. On the one hand, misunderstandings supposedly caused by linguistic or cultural mismatches can be used as excuses for problems in day-to-day activities. On the other hand, there is often a tendency to gloss over what seems to be a very 'soft' side of business. Even cordial, personal relationships with colleagues are no guarantee of thorough understanding in a business context. In this alone, the workshop was of huge value to us, and reflected what was happening also in our Practice Area Groups as individual lawyers faced up to the daily challenges of professional communications in an international environment.

Establishment of our values in the workshop was done through a process that sought to interpolate and validate them with reference to daily activities, judgements and decisions. Thus, relevance was built into them from the very beginning, and interpretation has become a matter of fleshing out the meaning and detail, not of controlling them to fit circumstances never considered. The way in which the vision, mission and values were used at the internal launch of the 'new' CMS will be dealt with later.

We also wanted the consultants to consider the name 'CMS', which was chosen early on without great regard to how it would be used later. They therefore first looked at the naming system to define criteria for the name, without prejudice as to whether CMS should be retained or a new name created. Law firms traditionally have long names, and the CMS member firms are no exception. No single firm was yet ready to forgo its existing name (indeed, the Germans even added a further name to their four-name blockbuster during the course of the project, although they have subsequently shortened it to CMS Hasche Sigle), but most were able to foresee the use of a common name at some point in the future.

Continuance of the existing names was therefore inevitable, somehow linked with the name of the 'Group' but, as we did not wish to give the idea that we were merely a loose association, a phenomenon quite widespread in the professional services world, the link had to be strong in order to express our vision and our intent to be eventually one practice. The name itself also had to be strong enough to perform its future function as a single identifier. This all led to the idea of a name as a prefix for the existing names, which would allow it to piggy-back onto a known name, gaining recognition value until the time came for it to stand on its own. The name would also have to be short and snappy, as well as usable around the world.

This is where 'CMS' came back into the picture. Whatever its weaknesses ('It sounds like the local boiler repairer', said one London partner, 'a compromise of the worst sort'), it was short and usable anywhere, even though there were various other CMSs in different businesses in different countries; and it already had some recognition value. In Germany the name had been well accepted, to the point of abbreviating office names to 'CMS Hamburg', 'CMS Stuttgart', and so on. This, we felt, had as much to do with the unwieldiness of the 'Hasche Sigle Eschenlohr Pelzer' name as it did with the good qualities of CMS, but in any case it was a step too far in that most other CMS firms would not countenance such usage for a considerable time.

Our consultants recommended retention of CMS because it filled the functional bill perfectly, and we would not have to go back to square one in terms of basic recognition. However, its role was redefined as a prefix for the existing names, only appearing 'solo' on communications descriptive of the whole organization, at least for the time being. Its sole use as the name for the organization, without the support of the existing names, is not yet envisaged and will only be implemented when the organization has achieved the target substance and recognition. In this way, the system responds truthfully to our development and is flexible enough to accommodate anticipated changes. Our aspirations are therefore presented credibly and the 'brand promise' of CMS is always met.

A corporate design

Because of the existence of two different corporate design styles within CMS (with further, smaller differences in the continental firms), the unification of this element had always been a principal aim of the project. Feelings on the subject ran highest in London, where the Cameron McKenna design, a rather unconventional one, had been widely embraced after initial strong resistance. In practical terms, it was not without problems – for example, faxing the logotype could be difficult – but even so it was only three years old, and to ditch it was seen as potentially destructive of the firm's identity, and wasteful. However, there was no question of adopting it (or something visually similar to it) for Europe-wide use, as there was widespread sensitivity to the possibility of London imposing its numerically superior, Anglo-Saxon will on everybody else. Indeed, the 'federal' structure of CMS had been identified as a major difference from other firms who had acquired in Europe, or merged. There was an existing

CMS mark, but it did not work satisfactorily in the context of the naming system and was somewhat equivocal in its symbology, to some people appearing as a partly-formed global projection, to others as confining the initials between a pair of parentheses.

Unlike the situation with the name, the consultants recommended a 'clean sheet' approach to the corporate design. They argued, successfully, that neither of the existing styles was suitable for our future visual representation and that, despite fairly strong feelings to the contrary in London, we should discard the Cameron McKenna corporate design for something entirely new. This, and the naming system, was to be a really major step in ramming home the CMS message internally, and particularly in London. Whereas, when CMS was first introduced, the logotype and some explanatory words were put onto the letterhead together with 'CMS Cameron McKenna' at a relatively small size, now the CMS branding would be unequivocal and inescapable. CMS would not be just an afterthought to Cameron McKenna, but an inseparable link to all other member firms.

It was just such an indication of commitment that was needed to put CMS on the map, both internally and externally. And, of course, it would have been difficult for any individual, or group of individuals, from any of the member firms to argue for such an action, since they would have been open to accusations of partisanship. The value of having outside consultants was proved in this, and other, matters.

The design process was not altogether straightforward. We had agreed the subjective associations we wanted to be projected: quality, dynamism, future orientation, confidence, integrity, openness and clarity. We were also made aware of the practical criteria such as legibility (especially important with our long firms' names), reproducibility at small sizes and on-screen, and so on. But the argument stuck at what was 'appropriate' for a law firm. It was the old thing about 'professionalism' again, and while in the UK we had become quite acclimatized to law firms having logotypes and symbols, it was a different matter in Germany.

There is an interesting aside at this point concerning the decision-making process. Our Executive Committee had been the natural and proper forum for decisions on this project, being composed of the most senior partners from the various offices. Just at the time when decisions needed to be made about the basic elements of the corporate design (the logotype, the colour and so on), the annual holiday season arrived and a number of senior partners departed. One or two of them sent deputies to the design presentations, and unfortunately the continuity was disturbed. The reason for mentioning this is to stress that this matter of branding, in total, is surely a question for the highest level of management, and certainly so in a professional services organization. It is also a matter for involvement and continuity, and it is key that the participants in the process follow it through as a team. Certainly, we found it difficult and delaying when others were delegated in to take decisions as part of a process they had not previously been involved with. On what basis could they make decisions? How could they feel the same sense of responsibility going forward?

Returning to the main theme: options were put forward by the consultants in an effort to find where the dividing line was between 'appropriate' and 'not appropriate'. At the same time, they pointed out that something that was so appropriate that it blended in with everything else was hardly likely to be a strongly differentiated solution. The discussion revolved around the typeface to be used, and the colour. Lawyers not generally versed in visual matters displayed great sensitivity on the precise thickness of letters and the exact shade of dark blue!

These international, multicultural negotiations eventually bore fruit, but the most convincing thing was when we were shown a representation of how the whole visual identity

C'M'S'

C'M'S' Lexcelis

C'M'S' Cameron McKenna

C'M'S' Bureau Francis Lefebvre

C'M'S' Carnogursky Strommer Reich-Rohrwig

C'M'S' Derks Star Busmann

C'M'S' Hasche Sigle

C'M'S' Strommer Reich-Rohrwig Karasek Hainz

C'M'S' von Erlach Klainguti Stettler Wille

C'M'S' Adonnino Ascoli & Cavasola Scamoni

The new CMS logotype, with the member firms, some of which have joined CMS since the branding project was carried out

C°M'S' Cameron McKenna

Banking and international finance

CMS Cameron McKenna is regarded as one of the pre-eminent firms in banking and international finance. We are among the few City firms with a large and experienced practice group able to meet clients' requirements in this specialist area. We act for more than 90 UK and international banks.

▸ **Areas of expertise**
▸ **Contact point**

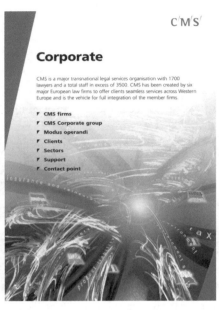

C°M'S'

Corporate

CMS is a major transnational legal services organisation with 1700 lawyers and a total staff in excess of 3500. CMS has been created by six major European law firms to offer clients seamless services across Western Europe and is the vehicle for full integration of the member firms.

▸ **CMS firms**
▸ **CMS Corporate group**
▸ **Modus operandi**
▸ **Clients**
▸ **Sectors**
▸ **Support**
▸ **Contact point**

C°M'S' Cameron McKenna

Rail

CMS Cameron McKenna is one of the leading legal firms specialising in transport and infrastructure development and restructuring. Our multi-disciplinary team can fully service the requirements of the worldwide transport industry.

▸ **International expertise**
▸ **Our services**
▸ **Contact point**

C°M'S' Cameron McKenna

Road transport

CMS Cameron McKenna is one of the leading legal firms specialising in transport and infrastructure development and restructuring. Through our global network of offices, our multi-disciplinary team can fully service the requirements of the worldwide transport industry.

▸ **Worldwide expertise**
▸ **Our services**
▸ **Recent experience**
▸ **Project management**
▸ **Contact point**

Brochures and leaflets strongly express the CMS corporate style

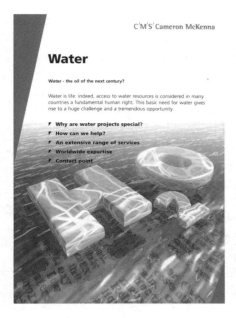

Water

Water - the oil of the next century?

Water is life; indeed, access to water resources is considered in many countries a fundamental human right. This basic need for water gives rise to a huge challenge and a tremendous opportunity.

▶ Why are water projects special?
▶ How can we help?
▶ An extensive range of services
▶ Worldwide expertise
▶ Contact point

scheme would look when applied to letterheads, business cards, printed matter, office signs and so on. Although we are aware that this is only the 'tip of the iceberg' as far as our brand identity is concerned, it was a most tangible expression of change and of our faith in CMS.

As mentioned earlier, CMS Cameron McKenna has its own in-house marketing department, and the marketing director had, of course, been a key member of the client side team on the project. At this point, we considered it would be helpful and desirable to involve our own designers, partly to get their seasoned views on the practicality of what was proposed, and partly to involve them in the planning for the impending internal launch and implementation. Much valuable information was gained in this way. It is amazing how a project of this type brings into question quite radical things in other areas, when standardization is being considered. The whole area of IT and systems is, of course, of key importance when discussing typefaces, layouts and colours, but also the way in which a report or proposal is structured and written is, if consistent, indicative of shared standards and a consistent delivery of quality of service.

This aspect received just enough attention at the time, in order to introduce standardized stationery across our firms, but much remains to be done. In any case, it is interdependent with matters of professional harmonization and service delivery, so is not something that can be dealt with in the short term. What is already clear, however, is that our vision, mission and values statement will have an influence in these areas, as it will in most aspects of corporate strategy.

I already referred to the tangible expression of identity which was so notable when we saw depictions of how the whole scheme would look. This sensation was heightened when we actually signed the first of our letters printed out on the new letterhead – which is getting a little too far ahead, because we first had to produce the guidelines and devise a strategy for the internal launch.

Our consultants explained the different types of corporate design guidelines which could be produced, at the same time recommending that the choice of medium should be based on who was to use the guidelines and exactly what information they needed. We discussed the idea of online guidelines and dismissed them as being too elaborate and expensive for our purposes. We opted for a limited quantity of printed guidelines, but with electronic files readily available. Templates were created for stationery and our office applications. In the meantime, the marketing department was busy preparing for launch day.

Not only were large amounts of pre-printed paperwork needed for 'the day', but all of the main templates had to be thoroughly proved, and further templates created for subsidiary applications. In London alone, nearly 60 leaflets and brochures were redesigned and printed in the new style, as direct replacements for the existing versions. Strictly speaking, as no name change was involved, it would not have been necessary to produce so much new material, but the decision was made to go all-out for impact, based on the fact that the CMS brand was at a turning point. If, at this stage, we did not carry everything through with utter thoroughness, professionalism and a sense of urgency, then our one chance to overcome past problems would be lost.

All the member firms accepted this, and plans and preparations were put in place in each country. When it came to the launch itself, we had to face a situation where, because of the widely varying conditions in the different firms – including basic size (50 people in Zürich, 600 people in London, for example), national and office cultures, state of internal communications development and so on – the strategy would have to respect and embrace specific conditions at a local level. London, however, presented the most complex situation because of a number of factors.

First, there was the question of numbers of staff, and the logistics of reaching them. Then, Cameron McKenna already had an overseas network with offices in places such as Hong Kong, Prague, Warsaw and Bucharest, which, quite apart from the CMS continental European firms, had to be incorporated into the process. Lastly, there was the London office culture. As remarked earlier, it was only three years since Cameron Markby Hewitt and McKenna & Co had merged and, at that time, a new visual identity had been produced and 'sold in' to some effect. When CMS was first introduced, it had been largely 'business as usual', with no change to the visual style, a rather subtle addition of the then-current CMS logotype, and day-to-day involvement restricted to those who were actively participating in CMS matters, which represented a rather small proportion of the whole. While recognizing that the visual element in all this is the 'tip of the iceberg', signing letters on a new letterhead which strongly proclaims 'CMS', which looks radically different from the previous and which is in the same style as those in, say, Zürich, is a hell of a signal that something has changed and that CMS now means business.

A new vision and values

However, apart from this superficial impact (relevant though it is), we had to remember that one of the original criticisms of CMS to date was that it lacked substance, that there was very little behind the brand. If we had decided simply to launch an alternative 'brand' (by which at this point I mean a corporate design style), we would have been ridiculed, or worse. The credibility gap between our original stated aims for CMS and reality would have widened to breaking point. It would, in fact, have been counter-productive, and our efforts to integrate and produce unity would have floundered. We therefore decided, on the consultants' recommendation, to use the vision and values as the basis of our communications.

When the workshop was carried out in Vienna, we had constructed our vision and values discussions around our day-to-day business experience and activities. We had started with broad discussions in order to reach a basis of understanding, then boiled down our long lists of aspirations and motivations to a compact, simple and straightforward vision statement, with a list of six single words or sets of words representing our core values. The vision statement we reached was:

> CMS aims to be a leading international provider of legal and tax solutions, committed to quality, the interests of its clients and the development of its people.

The values, at that time, were:

- client focus
- quality and integrity
- results-orientated
- entrepreneurial
- international
- partnership.

The vision was deliberately simple, bearing in mind the lack of clarity about CMS. The values were unpolished, but contained the essence of how we wanted to distinguish ourselves in our service and behaviour.

Inverting the process, to expand the descriptions of the values and bring them into relevance for day-to-day activities, was carried out by the Marketing Director in London. He had been present at the workshop, and so was entirely conversant with the context. An example of the result is the following explanation of our value 'client focus':

Client focus means
- exceeding client expectations
- developing bespoke solutions for clients
- identifying with individual clients' aims and concerns
- establishing enduring relationships with our clients based on mutual trust
- striving to add value to our service
- communicating with openness and clarity
- responding quickly to client requests
- seeking, listening to and acting upon our clients' feedback

- taking the lead in drawing issues to our clients' attention and recommending appropriate courses of action.

A launch strategy was devised for London, which featured the following. A generous area of office space was dedicated as a launch area, and a main room was set up to include a display of message panels, a refreshment bar and a corporate-blue sofa. The sofa featured as a theme in a video which was continually repeated.

Various partners and members of staff were shown seated on the sofa, reflecting and giving their own views on CMS, its vision and its values. In this way the relevance of the values to personal/professional situations was highlighted and emphasized. The room gave the opportunity for people to discuss reactions to the changes, and an adjacent room was fitted out with a video camera to record those reactions, if so desired. On overhearing some of the comments, one realized that, although not everyone liked the visual elements (surprisingly few did not), there was an overall thoroughness and professionalism about the presentation which was convincing and which showed that CMS was now a fully formed reality.

The newly designed and produced leaflets were on display, which made a tremendously impressive show. New signs were in place, and a booklet on 'Our new vision, values and identity standards' was distributed. This contained a general introduction, the vision statement, the full explanation of the values, and an explanation and illustrations of the new corporate design style. Also incorporated was a credit-card-sized version of the vision and values, for handy reference. The spirit of the whole exercise was effectively and stirringly summed up by CMS Managing Director, Pieter van Dalen, in his introduction:

> The adoption of a shared vision and common values is a milestone in the development of CMS.
>
> As a participant in the process that led to unanimous agreement on our vision and values, I was struck by the strength of common purpose amongst CMS member firms and the ease with which we were able to identify what is important to each of us – our values. If

anything, the difficulty lay in prioritizing our common values, rather than identifying them!

Our common identity standards are a further unifying factor; sending a clear message to our clients and the marketplace that we are all committed to CMS and that we speak with one voice.

In agreeing upon a vision, common values and identity standards, we have set a framework within which all CMS people can operate. The story does not end there, however. We have ambitious plans to build our cross-border practices and capabilities; to forge even closer links between member firms; and to offer our people greater opportunities to operate on a truly international level. Above all, we're setting in place structures to enable us to build upon our already considerable success in working with clients throughout Europe and beyond, in the spirit of true partnership.

Let's all focus on bringing our values to life and creating an organization of which we can be truly proud.

As Pieter implied, there is much still to do, but we have experienced extremely positive signs for the future. For example, just as we were finalizing the design process, our discussions with the top French firm, Bureau Francis Lefebvre, came to a successful conclusion. They took on board our vision, values and corporate design standards as a declaration and affirmation of belonging to the CMS family, and another important element of our shared global strategy was put into place.

What started as a 'corporate branding' exercise became a fascinating journey of self-discovery: not always comfortable, but enlightening and revealing. A sense of shared purpose is an essential basis for working towards a goal, but the goal has to be agreed first. We also learned (or had it confirmed) that a brand is not just a logo, or a set of brochures, or even the entire external appearance. The CMS brand is us. We live and breathe it, and it is expressed in all sorts of ways, formally and informally, externally and internally.

That CMS believes in its brand is now evident, and this is what will drive us forward in the process of achieving our vision.

The editors comment

CMS has demonstrated, without doubt, that superficial branding is not only of limited value in the short term, but can even be counter-productive in the long term. Without a cohesive and communicated vision, this pioneering project to build a pan-European legal services organization could not achieve its true potential, and was at risk of spreading scepticism within the member firms. The multi-cultural nature of the venture – which meant that firms who were new to each other had to deal with trans-national issues as well as the usual strains of integration – added another layer to the complexity of the situation. In making a courageous fresh approach to the branding issue, CMS brought life to its concept. This approach was followed through rigorously, from consultations with partners in all member firms, to the definition of a positioning statement and vision, mission and values, to internal communication of 'the big idea', then to guidelines for bringing the brand to life. CMS is aware that this has been a process of self-learning or, as Richard Taylor put it, 'an interesting journey'. However, the firm has now united under the CMS banner and is progressing its integration on a broad front, motivated by a common cause and a clearly-expressed goal.

Chapter 11
Continuity Through Change: Miele

Jürgen Plüss
Head of Business Unit, Kitchen Appliances International, Miele GmbH

Holistic Branding

Brand values are well on the way to becoming the predominant factor behind purchases of consumer goods. But which factors and instruments are suitable for building brand content and identity? The Miele case study proves that brand content for consumer goods can only really be effectively defined by adopting a holistic approach revolving around the product and its performance as the core elements. Furthermore, each redesign of brand identity must respect the current market perception of the brand. This restricts the scope for restructuring the values that are identical in terms of content. The rejuvenation and management of a brand is somewhat like attempting to dance with a straitjacket on.

What springs to mind when the name Miele is mentioned? On the one hand quality, dependability and durability, good service, innovations in the field of domestic appliances, convinced customers, conservative values, but on the other hand high prices and products that not everyone can afford. Products immediately associated with Miele are washing machines, dishwashers and vacuum cleaners. Although these top-of-mind values and products are by no means the only attributes and products the company has to offer, they are the ones that contribute most to perceived identity.

This comes as no surprise to experienced brand builders. The fact that brand tracking produces the same values and product ratings virtually all over Europe is the result of the company's 100-year history, and is confirmation of the theory that brand identity is always the result of a cumulative track record.

Miele: monopoly of quality values

The company's original objective of developing and selling only quality products with optimum functionality, unsurpassable dependability and durability at an appropriately high price level has been strictly adhered to since the company was founded in 1899. As a result, the Miele brand bears ample witness to the fact that a successfully implemented company philosophy has led to a 'quality' brand positioning, which, thanks to consistent action in keeping with this philosophy, enables Miele to monopolize values in the white goods market.

The core products in the history of Miele have always been those that emblazoned the word 'quality' in the minds of consumers. Washing machines and tumble dryers, dish-washers and vacuum cleaners are such products, favoured not so much as a result of creative adver-tising, unusual design or other communicative measures, but thanks to their sturdiness and dependability, their durability, innovative features, economical use of water and energy, modest, ageless, non-faddish design and good after-sales service.

Miele brand identity – current

Considering that market research shows that the motives for purchasing laundry care appliances have to do with discipline rather than emotions, the Miele brand's monopoly of quality values is the ideal prerequisite for Miele to become quality leader of the household appli-ance market.

Pricing and brand allegiance as a benchmark for qualitative market leadership

There are two key indicators of qualitative market leadership: on the one hand the extent of the price difference between a brand and its competitors, and on the other the repeat purchase rate.

On central European markets, the price for Miele products, for example washing machines or cylinder vacuum cleaners, is between 50 per cent and 70 per cent higher than that of competitor models. In Great Britain or Southern Europe, the difference may be as much as 100 per cent. These price gaps apply for products offering the same basic consumer benefits and similar features. The question arises here, as with similar premium brands in other areas, as to what it actually is that promises customers so much added value that they are prepared to pay 50 per cent more for a particular brand for an appliance with the same basic user benefits, comparable technical features and a design that, in some cases, is barely distinguishable from that of competitors. There is no pat answer in general, but in Miele's case, the willingness of consumers to pay more stems from the recognition that Miele products offer unbeatable product features, superb dependability and a 20-year life span. Miele products represent the best goods available in their category. In addition to these objective attributes, emotional values also play an important role. Their significance can only be measured on the basis of individual preferences. For example, what importance do consumers attach to knowing that they have bought the best, or that they have purchased a product that guarantees peace of mind? These values prompt purchasers to become Miele customers who, in their wish to purchase quality and their willingness to pay significantly more, are like-minded, regardless of their socio-demographic status.

Qualitative market leadership is also evident in the repeat purchase rate. This consumer–brand bond is also an expression of satisfaction. It can be assumed that the brand which enjoys the greatest customer satisfaction offers the best quality. Customer satisfaction may sometimes, however, be a questionable indicator, given the common definition according to which customer satisfaction is the difference between customer expectations and subjective perception. Given that customers expect Miele products to exhibit a high standard of quality to justify their premium price, even the slightest deviation from this standard will be a great disappointment. In other words, the high price and the excellent reputation the brand enjoys generate a positive preconceived image of the product in the consumer's mind. Even the slightest blemish, however, may tip the scales, with the effect that the consumer feels the product is not worth the price. It is therefore clear that consumers expect more of large and reputable brands, and these expectations are sometimes difficult to fulfil.

Even though consumer expectations of Miele products are high, brand allegiance is far greater amongst Miele purchasers than customers of other brands in the white goods industry.

Brand growth is restricted

Brands that are quality leaders in their respective markets generally operate in smaller segments. Premium segments tend to be smaller in volume, and are normally the preserve of one or two suppliers. As the premium supplier in the household appliance sector, Miele represents an exception to this rule. In significant areas of Europe, Miele dominates the markets for washing machines, tumble dryers and cylinder vacuum cleaners. This interesting combination of qualitative and quantitative market leadership completely contradicts the conventional price/quantity theory, and proves that concentration on top quality and high prices is not restricted to niche segments, but that in some markets volume in top price segments can be almost as significant as that at low price points. If Miele's market position were the norm, Mercedes-Benz would be market leader in the automobile sector, IWC in the watch-making industry or Bang & Olufsen in consumer electronics.

There is, however, one disadvantage in Miele's unique market position. Concentration on high-end price segments and leadership in significant markets mean that there is hardly any scope for growth. Profitability cannot be increased significantly (price gaps are already very high) and there is little room to expand Miele's position in these significant countries. If growth is one of the elements for survival, given today's competitive economy, then continuity – that is, company concentration on laundry care and cleaning appliances alone – is no longer a guarantee for further success through growth.

Continuity through change

The title of this case study, 'Continuity through change', now becomes clear to the reader. Continuity means adhering to tried and tested business patterns, whereas change implies something new. Is change not contradictory to continuity and the philosophy of remaining true to oneself, one of the basic rules of branding? The inclination is to answer this question in the affirmative, as each brand and each corporate identity has its limits. Brand management must take these limits, which also apply to what is actually expected of the brand, into consideration. A premium brand is severely restricted, for example with regard to distribution and pricing. Growth through retail presence and availability, for example in discount outlets or through conscious price erosion, is fatal for brand identity.

If a brand has exploited its potential to the full within its natural limits, the question of change or variation is not simply a theoretical marketing discussion, but becomes a matter of survival.

Growth without jeopardizing identity

For the Miele brand, the awareness that growth is necessary resulted in the identification and evaluation of strategic options that would ensure further sustainable growth without moving away from occupied brand values and market positions. Three strategic options were selected to deal with the problem of achieving growth without any fundamental change to core brand values. These options are a mixture of strategies to improve or optimize existing business processes and strategies to extend the range of activities:

- qualitative growth
- regional growth
- structural growth.

Options 1 and 2 are optimization strategies to achieve growth by improving margins through innovation and an increase in brand presence on regional markets outside Germany, particularly in Eastern Europe and overseas. Both strategies are based on traditionally achieved brand identity.

The third option is particularly challenging when dealing with Miele's brand identity, as it demands full penetration of all sales structures of the household appliance market, and not merely of the laundry care appliance sector. This strategic option appears highly attractive, not least since the 'cleaning' segment makes for only about 40 per cent of the market, leaving roughly 60 per cent potential for long-term, sustainable growth. Exploitation of this potential poses a great challenge, as it affects products that have a completely different ranking to laundry care appliances in the eyes of customers. These product structures involve appliances used for food storage and cooking.

Risk of identity hiatus through new product categories
Compared with laundry care appliances, which are utilitarian, the motives for using and purchasing cooking appliances are of a completely different nature. The focus here is not on sturdiness and durability, but on design, convenience of operation and functionality. Cooking appliances are sold through different distribution channels. They are displayed and sold predominantly by kitchen and furniture retailers, unlike washing machines which are mainly purchased from electrical retailers. This aspect is also of great significance, considering that traditionally, the main distribution channel for Miele products has been the electrical specialist dealer.

Important strategic resources must therefore be identified in order to develop new growth potential. These include the following:

- access to innovations
- access to distribution
- access to customers.

The first two resources are self-explanatory with respect to exploiting new potential. Access to innovation was given by the fact that products were already manufactured and developed in in-house facilities. Distribution resources on the other hand are easier to identify than to develop. Characteristic business practices and success factors in the kitchen and furniture retail trade had to be researched and implemented, even to the extent of taking on new staff.

The most effective and challenging resource in occupied and saturated markets is access to the customer. It is no longer sufficient to position the product itself in the appropriate distribution channels. An increasingly important success factor here is that the brand, together with the appropriate range of products, provides a convincing and harmonious package.

In the kitchen and cooking appliance sector it was necessary to overcome deficits in our approach to emotional issues such as pleasure, design and connoisseurship, which are essential for successful growth.

Incremental expansion of brand identity

The question now arises as to how new dimensions can be given to a brand with such a well-defined, clear-cut identity. Traditionally, communication agencies are consulted and assigned the task of giving new content to brand images and of communicating the new message.

This concept of brand development and management may be appropriate for certain consumer goods, but does not apply in the case of consumer durables. Brand building is an extremely complex and extenuated process which cannot be mastered by communicative measures alone. A brand is more than just a marque or logo, it constitutes the commonly accepted awareness and perception of the brand in the minds of customers. It is not logos or corporate colours that are decisive factors in competition, but the company behind the logo.

Miele brand identity – desired

Brand image and brand reputation are the result of a cumulative track record. Numerous factors contribute towards achieving this standing. In the case of consumer durables such as major electrical household appliances, quality, price, design, service, innovation, distribution and, without doubt, communication may all be instrumental in building brand image. A high degree of coherence – that is, a harmonious balance and long-term continuity without a hiatus in identity – is decisive in establishing a clear and lasting brand core.

Holistic branding must always incorporate product performance and innovation

In order to extend Miele's brand identity to include emotional values such as pleasure and connoisseurship, particular importance was attached to innovation, design and distribution as the key success factors. The most credible expression of brand identity is product performance. It is therefore not the traditional message that Miele stands for expertise and pleasure that changes the image of the brand, but rather actual proof in the form of innovation. Products are statements regarding performance which, in the long-term, join together to create a new image.

A wide range of innovations in the cooking and kitchen appliance sectors have indeed quickly brought Miele a high standing and acknowledgement in the appropriate distribution channels. This, in turn, is the key to customer access.

Access to new distribution channels was only possible thanks to a stream of innovations, some of which are illustrated here.

Miele built-in appliances with aluminium fronts. The elegance of these objects expresses technical and quality superiority in the kitchen

The credible expression of what a brand wants to be is innovation: this is exemplified by the world's first and only coffee maker for integration into kitchen units

Product design as a success factor is an expression of Miele's endeavours to occupy new product segments. Design is the embodiment of brand image: in other words, it must reflect consumer expectations and not send out conflicting messages. Familiarity, measured progression and consistency are the basic parameters of Miele design, which strives to be contemporary without overstepping the mark and becoming faddish.

In an age of increasingly interchangeable products and offerings, the theory that buyers purchase the brand and then the product is becoming more valid than ever before. Brands are therefore based on products and their performance, which should be in keeping with the image of the brand. If the brand promises too much, customers will become irritated and dissatisfied. If, however, a product exceeds expectations, consumers may still be taken aback, but the effect will be positive. The greatest effect is achieved when experience with a product confirms a preconceived brand image and strengthens existing perceptions in the consumer's mind. And strong brand perception, in turn, offers a well-guarded defence against attacks from competitors. In this respect Miele stands as an example for an optimistic approach to growth based on the management and cautious extension of brand identity through highly efficient products.

Holistic branding integrates all influences on brand perception

Nowadays, the motives for purchasing consumer durables such as watches, furniture, motor cars and electrical household appliances have to do with brand emotion. The more the basic benefit of a product is offered in a similar quality and with the same degree of durability by several different brands, the greater influence the brand has as an ambassador of social and emotional values. Emotion, however, needs a foundation not provided by advertising or attractive design, but by the brand core, the product itself.

There is no doubt that in the market for consumer durables, products and services are the best expression of what a company or a brand strives or aims to be. This perception is the focus of the Miele case study. There are, however, additional success factors which influence or help to create the identity of a brand in the market for consumer durables.

A brand needs a heritage

How many brands can claim that the advertising slogans promoting its products 76 years ago are still used today? Miele can.

Miele also cultivates its history by maintaining Europe's largest domestic appliance museum, which is open to the public. Exhibits from the family history, which at the same time reflect the history of household appliances, are available on loan for exhibitions and are a constant reminder to the general public of the richness of Miele's past. Miele uses its past as active capital to foster the aura of the white goods pioneer.

A brand needs appropriate distribution channels

If you want to purchase a high-quality watch, where do you go to buy it – to a department store, discount store, mail-order company, Internet shop or specialist dealer? It is obvious that a certain category of quality products or quality brands does not have such a variety of options as products marketed through multi-channel distribution systems. The temptation to succumb to the growth trap posed by inappropriate distribution channels is great. Evidence that competitors' goods are sold there should not distract brand managers from the fact that certain brands would be in danger of losing their reputation for quality if they were sold through inappropriate distribution channels. A distribution channel that does not offer a suitable market backdrop, does not offer an adequate expert advisory service and cannot provide a delivery and commissioning service cannot argue that the asking price for the product is justifiable. This then triggers off the call for lower prices which, in turn, leads to a reduction in quality as costs have to be cut in order to meet these price demands.

Every brand has its limits and it is important to keep within them, even when it comes down to distribution. In our case this means that Miele products are only distributed by specialist dealers or by retailers offering similar services.

A brand needs the right purchasers

Purchasers are brand ambassadors. This applies to all products and services offered – for cars, restaurants and tourist regions alike. As a rule, a company has a precise conception of the targeted purchasing group and of individual preferences regarding services, design, point of purchase and price. A brand searches for and finds its customers and vice versa. Target group orientation means concentration on limited market segments and accepting their limits. The situation becomes problematic for brand managers when the natural limits of target group potential have been reached and aspirations are for further growth. In this event, the brand must open up to additional target groups. This opening up or extension of the brand seldom fails to have an adverse effect on regular customers or users, causing them to break ties with their brand and look elsewhere.

Design spearheading brand expansion: Miele's TopCook cooking range, with a semi-professional look and appropriate performance.

In this respect, the Miele brand is managed with great sensitivity. It is essential to know your customers well if you wish to maintain the attraction of a brand in the eyes of its regular target group. It is essential that loyal customers are not upset, and this demands unwavering recognition and assertion of the brand's dos and don'ts. This knowledge is a valuable asset for a good brand manager.

A brand needs a perfect service network

For many consumer goods, no great importance is attached to customer service. In the case of consumer durables, however, service is an extremely important instrument which can strengthen or weaken the competence of a brand.

If brand reputation is the result of a cumulative track record, experiences with after-sales service may play a decisive role in achieving this record. Service incidents are annoying and weaken brand loyalty. If, however, faults or signs of wear and tear do not occur until several years into a product's useful life, brand ties may even be strengthened. After-sales service that is easily accessible, readily available, friendly, competent and efficient when dealing with problems, underpins a positive brand image. In this context, the words often quoted by spokespeople from the motor industry, 'Each service incident offers the opportunity to prove the efficiency of our company', are not without truth, provided after-sales service processes function perfectly.

Service incidents are part of relations management between a company and its customers. The intensity and nature of this relationship will become even more important in the future than it is now. Passive media such as classical advertising are being supplemented more and more, and may even be gradually replaced in the future, by active dialogue-oriented media, such as loyalty clubs and the Internet. An outstanding after-sales service organization with its manifold opportunities for dialogue with the customer is a constituent part of such a relations chain.

As consumer durables are subject to wear and tear, Miele has to prove its value as a quality brand through the after-sales service offered during a product's lifecycle. In many markets Miele has the largest after-sales service organization in its field. If this service network can then satisfy customers in the event of a fault, the consumer–brand bond will be strengthened.

In some markets the service culture that distinguishes Miele even goes as far as offering evening and weekend appointments for service calls. Premium brands covering purchasing groups with customers of a high social standing must be extremely versatile here to ensure that after-sales service achieves the same success as other instruments that have an impact on the brand.

A brand needs the right price

Apart from the strategic issues that influence price definition – the sales volume and production capacity to be achieved, which other product levels and prices have to be considered, on which markets the product is to be placed – the question as to what is the right price may be answered differently by sales, accounts or marketing. This difference in approach within a company however, is not the issue here; it merely represents an idiosyncrasy within each organization. A new aspect should be considered: the interplay between brand and price.

Brand and price are not independent of each other, as is shown in a comparison between a 5-series BMW with a 2.5 litre 6 cylinder engine and an Opel Omega with the same engine. The price difference between these two offers, which are basically the same in form, is around 30 per cent. Obviously it can be said that these two vehicles are not comparable, but they are when it comes down to their core offer and basic benefits. It can be said, however, that an Opel offered at the price of a BMW would never find a buyer and a BMW for the price of an Opel would confound the buyer. The same applies to Miele. The price for Miele products is between 50 per cent and 100 per cent higher than that of competitor models. Apart from the fact that the additional benefits and longer lifecycle justify this price difference, the high price testifies to the expectation of a higher quality. The feeling for value born from experience that quality, particularly first-class quality, can never be achieved at a low price obviously has an impact on brand perception. A low price can cause great irritation for a brand that has quality as its core strength, since the consumer's positive preconception that good quality means a high price is spoilt by this experience. A high price on the other hand confirms the cumulative track record for quality. For economic reasons and for the sake of their reputation, brands that stand for quality and offer added benefits accordingly can never be price leaders. In the short term, brand managers who break this rule will register an increase in sales, but in the long term, down-trading will ruin the added-value aspect and lead to a loss of the core expression of brand identity, which is quality.

A brand needs correct corporate behaviour

The influence of the appearance and behaviour of a company and its representatives on a brand should not be underestimated. As already mentioned, brands enjoy a preconceived image in the minds of the customer. If corporate behaviour complies with this image, opinions and preconceptions are consolidated. A company manufacturing and selling sports equipment, for example, should publicly campaign for sport, or its representatives should appear to be actively engaged in sport. This kind of self-promotion can be applied specifically to many brands and meets with widespread acceptance. When dealing with some general issues, however, companies lack public sensitivity, as shown by the example of environmental protection which does not permit companies to make the mistake of adopting a different viewpoint from the general consensus. Environmental protection, safety, quality, customer orientation and dependability are values that govern Miele's activities, and are in line with the image of the brand and its products. It is also considered extremely important that managerial staff are involved in social and cultural activities outside the company, not only because this involvement broadens the horizon of the personnel involved, but also because it contributes to presenting the company and the Miele brand as a responsible and committed part of the community.

A brand needs success

It is surprising how seldom the success factor is considered worth mentioning in literature on brand image. The choice of a specific brand will always consciously or subconsciously answer the question, 'What does the brand say about me?' A brand that enjoys economic success and communicates this fact increases its attraction compared to competitors with less success.

Economic difficulties can result in a loss of desirability even for emotionally stable brands such as Porsche, as was the case when the exchange rate for the US dollar was low in the mid-1980s, causing a downturn in sales on the then dominant US market.

A brand needs communication

According to communication agencies, communication is the main factor for brand building or the perception of a brand. Admittedly, this may apply to certain consumer goods such as cigarettes. In the markets for consumer durables, however, communication is just one of many success factors. A good quality product, correctly distributed and offered at an appropriate price point, can be successful without any great promotional effort. However, this applies to products more than brands.

As brands are aimed at different socio-economic groups, they need communication to confirm the needs of their target groups and ensure that the brand is publicly seen to retain its attraction. Miele has opted for a style which is virtually the same all over the world, using the colour blue to highlight technical precision and quality, and focusing on product performance without any distracting emotional elements. Admittedly, such campaigns would not win any prizes for creativity in competitions. They do, however, present a composed brand image and confirm consumer expectations of the brand without any irritating aspects.

A change of strategy generates fierce resistance

The results on which this case study is based (situation: high degree of market penetration = reduced growth potential; objective: exploitation of new market segments = basis for further growth) corresponded to the simple logic of GAP analyses, as usually applied by management consultancies, central corporate planning departments or marketing divisions. This means, in simple terms:

- identification, analysis and evaluation of status quo
- definition and specification of target status
- analysis and specification of gaps between actual and target status

- analysis, development and definition of activities to overcome defi-
  ciencies.

If they are performed accurately, GAP analyses represent a comprehen-
sible and validated train of thought with a compelling logic which
encourages wide acceptance and a dedicated implementation of strategies. Experience has shown, however, that the more radically strategies
attempt to change a company's way of thinking and behaviour, the
fiercer the opposition, since change is not welcomed by every employee
and department. Logically, immediate action may be called for, but as
long at it entails a different way of thinking and new behaviour patterns,
the implementation of a strategy may be faced with a great deal of
tenacious opposition. This may be acceptable, provided it simply
complicates or slows down the implementation process. If, however, this
opposition actually prevents strategies from being implemented, it
could have serious consequences for the development of the company.

Resistance to new strategies is particularly fierce when a company or
brand is enjoying success. Experience has shown that comprehension of
the need for change is greater when a company is floundering. The
perception of Bertelsmann proprietor Reinhard Mohn that a company is
well advised to question and change its strategy when still thriving has
been quoted more than it has been actually put into practice. This
concept is correct, however, since a thriving company has the time and
capital thoroughly to prepare and implement change. Changes can only
be achieved if supported by company directors and appreciated and
accepted by senior and middle management. This was the case at Miele,
where acceptance was encouraged by the dramatic shift in currency
exchange rates in the first half of the 1990s. This led to a significant dete-
rioration in export opportunities for German products which could not
be compensated for by higher growth on the home market. Hence the
options for Miele growth, which were focused on foreign growth, were
reduced and a new evaluation of growth potential was called for. Against
this backdrop, a new strategy also propagating growth on the home
market, in this case the largest household appliance market in Europe,
had to be communicable and perceivable.

Brand management must always be measured by economic success

The case study would not be complete if there were no evidence of its success. The final charts indicate market developments for household appliances, subdivided into freestanding and built-in appliances, compared with Miele's development as a whole. Whereas the limited potential for growth is obvious in the case of traditional freestanding appliances (Miele index 126 compared with market 117), Miele has achieved above-average growth compared with market development

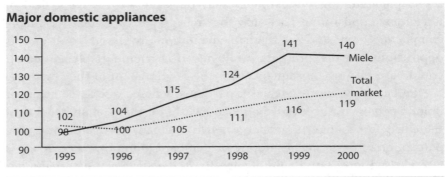

Major domestic appliances

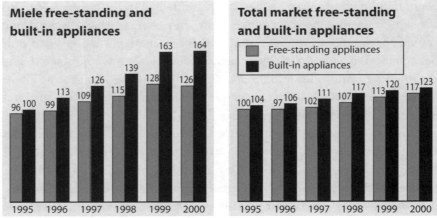

Miele free-standing and built-in appliances

Total market free-standing and built-in appliances

Miele's sales development for major domestic appliances, Europe.
Index: units in %. Basis: 1994 = 100%.

in the built-in appliance sector (Miele index 164 compared with market 123).

This development is both confirmation and incentive for the continued cultivation and measured expansion of Miele's brand identity through holistic brand management, incorporating product performance and services.

The editors comment

Brand strength is key at times of change. One of our other cases – BUPA – is concerned with repositioning the brand in total, whereas the Miele case is a perfect example of brand stretch, or extension. Faced with a situation where the only growth option was to enlarge its range of products, Miele decided to conceive, design, develop and market the new product ranges in accordance with its established, and highly positive, brand values. In doing so, it was necessary to restate its values, for the benefit of those within the company who would be dealing with formerly 'non-Miele' product ranges, those in the distribution chain and for customers. In all of this, Miele had even to beware of cultural differences which exist between those who deal with, on the one hand, washing machines and, on the other hand, cooking appliances. This was in addition to basic consumer attitudes, where, for example, washing machines are viewed as 'utility room' objects, whereas cookers are viewed more as a style statement. Such a holistic, and detailed, view of all factors that could possibly influence the brand extension brought dividends in terms of the growth actually achieved. The whole case neatly demonstrates the application of holistic thinking to an area of branding which would traditionally have been considered only as a marketing task.

Chapter 12
Rejuvenating a Proud Brand: Dunlop Sport

Graeme Derby
Group Marketing Director, Dunlop Slazenger International

We believe we can

There are very few brands that survive for over 100 years, never mind remain strong contenders in their market. Dunlop Sport is one of these, but it is clear that firm action is required to ensure that the brand, so popular in the twentieth century, will still be competing well into the twenty-first. The story of Dunlop Sport's rejuvenation – a process which is still work in progress – is one of a company which has been prepared to turn its brand, its belief and its behaviour inside out, to make sure of its future.

To understand Dunlop's brand mission in the twenty-first century, you have to understand its context: the growth of sports and consumers'

The breakthrough dodecahedron (DDH) pattern golf ball of 1979, a Dunlop first

The well-known Dunlop 'D', used for everything from tyres to rackets

involvement in brands which have been such a significant part of life in the last 20 to 30 years. Tennis and golf have developed from low-key, participative sports for the leisured and monied, to mass participation sports which are also global commercial undertakings, watched by millions of people live and on television around the world. Players have become some of the world's wealthiest individuals, celebrities who frequent the gossip columns and are called on to endorse products from watches to cars. Riding this wave has been one of Dunlop's challenges: the brand has to keep up to stay in business.

Dunlop's development was also influenced by another trend. The business itself was a victim of the acquisition and merger strategies so prevalent during the 1980s. Its renaissance is important for the management who owns the business, the banks that finance it and indeed to the country, as Dunlop is one of the last surviving major British-owned sports brands.

The case history that follows is of a brand in transition: rejuvenating itself to meet existing and new challenges, redefining itself by understanding its consumers and building a brand positioning which permeates the business. We have a lot to do but we believe we will be successful. Or as our then European Managing Director, Andrew Griffiths, said at the start of this process, 'We can because we believe we can!'

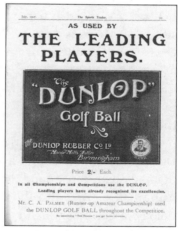

Dunlop enters sport, via the golf ball, in 1907

From unusual beginnings

The Dunlop sports business had an unusual start in that it was born from the Dunlop Pneumatic Tyre Company Ltd, which had first established itself in Dublin in 1889. It was not until 1909 that the company realized the potential for another use of rubber, the golf ball. Golf had grown in popularity during the nineteenth century with the formation of local clubs, and the Royal and Ancient at St Andrews became the supreme authority on the rules of the game in 1919.

Dunlop introduced the first tennis racket in 1917 and a separate sports business, the Dunlop Sports Company, was formed in 1928. The Maxply name that has become famous in tennis circles entered the Dunlop portfolio in 1931, with the launch of the Maxply Fort. In that year, 42 Wimbledon players used Dunlop rackets and six out of the eight Italian Open finalists also played Dunlop. The Dunlop tennis ball was advertised as being responsible for Britain's victory in the Davis Cup. In golf too, Dunlop was associated with success. Henry Cotton, British Open Golf Champion, endorsed Dunlop golf balls in the 1930s.

After the First World War, Dunlop had embarked on a period of rapid expansion around the world using its expertise in rubber technology, largely following in the footsteps of the British Empire. Dunlop established multi-product factories, usually based around the initial tyre plant. Countries like Australia, South Africa, Canada, France and Japan were lucrative markets as sports were demonstrating the same rapid growth as in the UK. As interest in

5628   T4121

DUNLOP RACKETS
at Wimbledon

Forty-two Players at Wimbledon used Dunlop Rackets. Of these twenty-eight were National Champions or Davis Cup Players.

Dunlop Tennis Rackets are rapidly achieving the popularity they deserve.

In the Italian Championships 6 out of 8 finalists used Dunlop Rackets, and 3 events were won with these famous rackets, whose excellence and reliability are amply confirmed by their overwhelming success at Wimbledon.

An advertisement from 1931

Dunlop SPORTS SHOES
4 OUT OF 5 WIMBLEDON PLAYERS WEAR THEM

In 1958, four out of five Wimbledon players wore Dunlop sports shoes

sports increased, so the operations grew and began to introduce other products. By 1946 the business was marketing a number of products for tennis, badminton and squash: rackets, presses, balls and shuttles, nets, posters, court equipment and footwear. For hockey: sticks, balls and boots. For golf: balls and footwear. In additional the product range included dartboards, cricket balls, medicine balls, gymnasium mats and various other accessories.

In 1959 the Dunlop International Sports Company acquired the Slazenger Group, although the two brands remained separate, and still today Slazenger rackets compete, largely in the UK market, against the bigger and more international Dunlop brand.

The sports business was run separately from the tyre business, going through several ownerships before its restructure in 1985, and the takeover by BTR in 1986. Then all the Dunlop-owned sports businesses were pulled together to form Dunlop Slazenger International Ltd, with a single management team responsible for worldwide sports operations. For the first time

Wimbledon champion Lew Hoad declares
his preference, 1961

John McEnroe and
the Maxply in 1981

there was a single entity that directed the worldwide resources and performed a coordination function for research and development, manufacturing and marketing. It also enabled rationalization and the eradication of some duplication: for example at one time there were seven company-owned factories manufacturing tennis balls, competing in a global market which today is only worth £300 million. However true global reach was lost, as Dunlop had divested its operations in Australia, New Zealand, Japan and France. The new company was marketing four main brands: Dunlop, Slazenger, Maxfli (golf balls) and Carlton (badminton).

The Dunlop brand had always publicized itself, and improved its customer perception, by sponsoring leading players who used and endorsed its products. Martina Navratilova, Yvonne Goolagong, Virginia Wade, Rod Laver and Lew Hoad were tennis greats and ambassadors for the brand who used Dunlop in the 1960s and 1970s. In 1981 Dunlop scored a major coup in signing the high profile, if volatile, John McEnroe, a famous sportsman and huge celebrity. Tony Jacklin, Arnold Palmer, Peter Thomson and Bernhard Langer all used Dunlop golf balls. In squash too, the Maxply Fort brand made its mark, with all the British Championship winners using Dunlop rackets in 1967, and Geoff Hunt winning the first Squash World Championship with Dunlop racket and balls. However, the business suffered from lack of continuity of management and consistency of behaviour. The company backed off from promotion and investment. The Sports Company was the only consumer goods business in an industrial conglomerate and it showed.

During the late 1980s, the company lost direction. The player portfolio became weak. During the 1970s and early 1980s, Dunlop had been synonymous with top tennis and golf professionals, but between 1984 and 2002 the company did not have one male Grand Slam winner using its rackets. Steffi Graf was signed to the company as a young player, but when she began to do well, the attitude was to reduce her retainer as she was winning so didn't need it! Dunlop was slow to recognize the potential of new materials, believing that wood would remain dominant. Today, no rackets are made of wood.

In 1996 the business was bought by its management, led by the venture capitalist, CinVen, and a consortium of banks led by NatWest. The company is now private, with 51 per cent of the equity held in trust. The company currently employs 1,800 people, and has sales of around £120 million. It has significant businesses in the UK, the United States, the major European countries and the Asia Pacific region. It was time to retrench, reconsider and rejuvenate.

The rejuvenation team

> This team is the epicentre for the emotional revival of the Dunlop brand.
>
> Phil Parnell, Chief Executive

In 1999, Dunlop rejuvenation was decreed to be the number one global priority for the organization. The critical decision to embark on a programme of rejuvenation was not a marketing exercise. It was driven from the Chief Executive's office and was more than just tinkering with the brand. The intention was a root and branch examination of the brand and its positioning, the company culture and behaviour, and how they communicated the Dunlop vision both internally and externally. A steering committee was brought together which included marketing, logistics, finance, sales, human resources and manufacturing, and it was this team that drove the project. It was responsible for:

- overall strategic direction
- reviewing progress of the work
- selecting and managing consultants.

A further 20 senior and middle managers, drawn from across functions and territories, formed action teams, and fed information about their specific areas into the steering committee. They were a sounding board for the plans that were developed, and were to act as ambassadors when the message was finally cascaded to the rest of the company.

The involvement of such a multi-disciplinary, multi-skilled group ensured that developments were rooted in practicality and deliverable to the rest of the business. With the CEO as project champion, the management of the project was the job of the marketing department, which acted as the hub for gathering information and generating ideas and drove the project through.

It was decided to focus first on tennis in the UK, being the biggest sports sector and the home market. Learnings would then be shared and extended to other markets with minor adaptation. The plan took nine months to bring to fruition, and the steering committee met approximately every month. Each meeting was followed with a newsletter to members of the action teams, with a progress report. They would then give feedback on developments and suggestions. Once the plan was finalized, it was introduced to the rest of the company in a series of big events where the new positioning was explained.

The health of the brand at the beginning of the project

The two main product areas for Dunlop are golf and tennis. Tennis accounts for around 60 per cent of sales revenue, made up of rackets and balls. Golf balls, clubs and accessories are responsible for 33 per cent of sales, and the remainder is from squash rackets and balls. A realistic assessment of the current status of the brand and its position in the market revealed:

- Brand positioning was fragmented and inconsistent. For example, in the UK Dunlop was associated with old-fashioned wooden rackets, whereas in Germany it had a high-quality premium position.
- However the brand did have over 100 years of heritage and was recognized as a major player in tennis, golf and squash.
- Product ranges were inconsistent in positioning and imagery.
- The company did not have a full understanding of the motivations of its consumers and what they were looking for.
- The player portfolio had been reduced; major players were signed to competitors.
- The company did not have a pool of up-and-coming, talented players who would be tomorrow's role models.

- However, Dunlop can still claim that more tennis Grand Slams have been won with its rackets than any other brand.
- Young people generally have a lot of other leisure pursuits than sport competing for their attention and money.
- There was a lack of a unifying cohesion within the company; no consistency of vision between different divisions and areas.
- People were no longer confident about Dunlop's success because of a history of false starts. The challenge was to change people's focus and begin to believe in the new vision.
- There were conflicting agendas and no real brand champion.
- The company was inward-looking and, in some ways, still tied to its industrial past.
- And the competition was becoming bigger and stronger.

The competition
There is a number of sports equipment companies such as Callaway, Wilson and Head, that are traditional direct competitors of the brand. There are niche players in each sport who offer specialist products. However, a new challenge is coming from the global sports companies such as Nike, Adidas and Reebok. These companies, originating in maybe one or two sports sectors, first made the transition into the everyday and fashion apparel categories. In their search for new markets, they are expanding into the equipment sector and turning to new sports. Already Nike has sourced golf equipment and, with its deep pockets, launched with a multi-million sponsorship of Tiger Woods, one of the most successful golfers today.

The worldwide market
The market for tennis rackets is currently worth £180 million, tennis balls £120 million, golf clubs £2.3 billion and golf balls £960 million. The markets are driven by a need for new products, although this is often more line extensions, rather than genuine innovation. All manufacturers will replace the majority of their product range every year. Both customers and trade now expect it.

The price of a tennis racket varies between £20 and £200, and prices have remained static for the last 20 years. Products are distributed through specialist outlets, club shops and sports retailers, ranging from proprietor-owned single units to multiple chains.

While golf is growing in popularity, in the UK, British tennis players' poor performance in recent years, lack of facilities and competition from other sports or leisure activities have led to a decline in interest and participation. However there is a still a great deal of interest in the sport, and long-term decline seems to have stabilized.

The consumer

The target market for most mass-production sports equipment manufacturers is the committed amateur who makes up 80 per cent of the sales. The 'halo' effect is a significant factor in the sports equipment market. People want the reassurance of using the same equipment as their heroes, their coaches and to some extent their peers. Price, style and performance are important in making the decision, but possibly come into play once the brand has been selected.

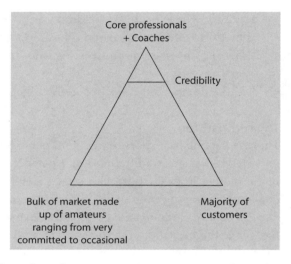

Attitudes to Dunlop

Dunlop is considered as a 'second tier' brand by consumers in general, with brands like Nike, Reebok and Adidas in the Premier Division. It currently has low unprompted awareness. However, this is not a major concern as we do not believe that general consumer research and tracking will be of value to the brand. Our heartland lies in the small sector of the population who play our sports, and those are the people who we need to reach.

To the over-35 age group, we believe Dunlop probably means John McEnroe and the 'green flash' sports shoes which were once as ubiquitous among UK teenagers as Nike and Reebok are today. The under-35s have a less strong association with the brand, but more importantly, no emotional baggage or negatives.

The solution

- Use research and imaginative analysis to reposition the brand.
- Create a new positioning and vision.
- Identify a new target audience and hone our marketing and product development towards this group.
- Get under the skin of consumers' reasons for playing sport, and find ways of identifying with and demonstrating our understanding of their needs.
- The more 'emotional' the insight, the more persuasive the proposition.
- Create a vision and cultural identity that the company can live and breathe.
- Make the brand work from inside out – bring the strategy to life.

Developing the new vision

Research and analysis

We have significantly improved our understanding of the market and the critical consumer groups for Dunlop by holding three-hour focus group sessions with 50 people in many territories. We consulted with top players and coaches. There is a temptation to believe that the consumer is interested in the technology behind the brand. What we found was exactly the opposite. Technological distinctiveness is only a powerful driver for purchase when consumers believe the brand understands their needs and desires in playing sport. The research helped us to understand how to express the benefits Dunlop Sport offers consumers, and gave us guidance on our crucial positioning work.

A significant finding was that the consumer in all our markets is very similar at the emotional level. A key learning was that sport is all emotion. Our consumers believe that sport is all about effort, concentration and sheer determination. The more you put in, the greater the elation when it all pays off. And the deeper we demonstrate that we understand this, the more people will believe in our product excellence. Very few sports brands understand this, and it gave us a new sense of confidence that there was still a lot of residual value and potential in the brand. We moved forward prepared to act like leaders, not followers.

Who are we selling to?

Our target audiences are primarily the 25–30 year old male (as more men play sport regularly than women do), and the opinion formers in that group. We are targeting the 'avid' player who makes up 25 per cent of consumers, yet accounts for 50 per cent of the sales in value. As the piechart shows, avid amateur players who play golf or tennis more than 21 times a year are very similar in the share they take of sales.

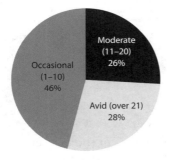 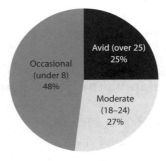

Number of times/rounds of tennis played a year in the USA
Total players over 12 years old: 19.2 m

Number of rounds of golf played a year in the USA
Total players over 12 years old: 26.4 m

Segmenting the market to get a clearer picture

We realized that knowing our consumers intimately was the key to securing our market share and growing the brand. Without this knowledge we did not think we could get close enough to the consumer's thinking to really make a difference. This work involved looking at motivation from several different aspects and developing a series of hypotheses from which we could build our strategy. We created maps that showed how the flow of influence on purchase could be tracked between different groups. We concentrated on three key lifestage moments when players can move from recreational to avid players.

Recreational players

We can identify two types of these:

- People just starting to play who may already have, or who could gain, the desire to play more regularly and improve, and may have the ability to become good players.
- Those who have a low motivation to improve, being satisfied with their level of involvement.

Recreational players have the choice whether to stay as they are, possibly improving just because they are playing, or to make a conscious decision to go actively for improving their game. Then they become competitive, win-orientated, not just doing it for the exercise or the social networking. They are looking for external recognition for their success.

Progressive improvers

These are the people who are facing a decision about how much they are prepared to commit in order to improve and achieve success. They are on the threshold of a higher level of mental, physical and emotional involvement with the sport. They may have become involved and wedded to the sport or just want to strive for personal satisfaction.

The elite

This final 'amateur' group are those who are just below the higher echelons of professionals, top coaches and top amateurs. Their decision point is whether they want to join the elite or are content to play at a high level and can receive sufficient personal satisfaction from this.

We created a map of the functional, rational and emotional motivations for sport – a 'Sports Needscape' – as demographic analysis would provide little help in targeting the opinion formers mentioned earlier. Our Needscape demonstrated how progression is a core driver for participation in sport,

'Sports Needscape': a map of the functional, rational and emotional motivations for sport. 'Progression' is a core driver.

Transcendence
Actualisation

Personal Mastery
Fulfilment
Vision
Leadership
Inspiration
'Winning'

Self-expression
Creativity
Flair, finesse
Touch
Inventiveness
Perfection

Pleasure
Well-being
Satisfaction
Rhythm
Style
Balance

Special (high talent/ skill)

Achievement
Challenge
Commitment
Determination
Power control

Personal Values
Striving
Momentum
Resilience
Courage
Self-belief
Willpower

Compete (result)

Performance
Skill
Sweat/effort
Testing limits
Technique
Strength
Dynamism

Progression
Improvement
Confidence
Concentration
Goals

Fun
Sociability
Relationships
Participation
Inclusion
Image

Participate (experience)

Fitness
Stimulation
Excitement
Ability
Physique

Play
Recreation
Leisure

Everyday/ ordinary (basic skill)

Health
Activity
Energy
Stress/tension release
Displacement

which in turn affects purchase of equipment. As players achieve more mastery – both personal and physical – so their propensity to play regularly increases.

Levels of involvement with sport vary. There is a scale of involvement which tracks from low involvement and participation, where the emotional response is low, to high involvement, where people are deeply involved with the physical, mental and emotional aspects of the game.

Understanding the consumer

Through our brand immersion research we identified seven key insights:

The intense personal inner-directed highs of sport motivate everybody.

Power, aggression and beating your opponent motivate some (less confident) players – but alienate everyone else.

Ultimate sport is all about effort, determination, concentration and the absolute elation when this pays off.

Nobody owns this emotional high ground. The assumption is that it must be Nike!

The simple act of demonstrating this understanding will add performance credibility to the equipment.

Implies Dunlop has physically and emotionally tested its equipment and that it is endorsed by professionals.

Players know ability counts for far more than their equipment *and* they feel being told different 'is talking down to them'.

Performance-based claims can easily come across as unbelievable or patronizing.

People forget all about their equipment when they are playing well. It just feels like part of them.

It becomes a physical and emotional extension by responding to the way they are already playing.

However people would like more help choosing the right equipment 'for them and their game' in store.

Doing so would demonstrate Dunlop's responsiveness to customer needs.

The brand does not carry too much baggage to do this.

But we will have to do it for real in terms of novelty, authenticity and attention to gritty reality.

Who does our consumer take a lead from?

Opinion formers are very significant in our market. In particular, those who we describe as the 'elite' – professionals, coaches and top amateurs – will have an impact most particularly on the next level down of regular committed players, but also affect everyone involved in the sport. Lower down the playing hierarchy, players will also be affected by those just above them in ability as well as their peers. So top club players can influence the rest of the members, who see their use of particular equipment as an endorsement, and perhaps an indication that they themselves could generate a better performance if they upgraded their own rackets or balls.

The concept which informed our strategy: 'digging deeper'

In brand immersion workshops, we tested a number of consumer propositions:

Winning edge:	'We give you the winning edge'
Invisible coach:	'We help you take your game to new levels'
Powerful weapons:	'We give you the power to crush your opponent'
Complete control:	'We put you in complete control of the game'
On fire:	'We give you the confidence to keep going for winners'
Emotional roller coaster:	'The emotional roller coaster of sport drives everything we do'
Magic moments:	'We inspire the thrill'
Digging deeper:	'We help you dig deeper when it matters most.'

It was the 'digging deeper' concept that resonated most and that has helped us form our vision and strategy.

What is 'digging deeper'?

We all recognize those nerve-jangling moments when we're coming down to the wire – facing defeat or in danger of choking at match-point or the winning putt.

> These are the times you need to find inner reserves of determination and self-belief.
>
> We help you dig deeper when it matters most.
>
> We understand what it is like to be severely tested and to come through the fire.
>
> You can have total confidence in our equipment to respond whatever demands you put on it.
>
> It is play tested under the most extreme physical, mental and emotional conditions.'

Company vision

> To reinstate Dunlop as a leading multi-sports brand.

There is no benefit to being a niche market, or one-dimensional brand. The challenge will come from the major sports companies whose brands are strong enough to cross boundaries between sports, between sport and fashion and across age groups. Once, as our past has shown, Dunlop had that ability. We are determined to seek it again.

Brand vision

> Dunlop will inspire a new generation of committed younger sports players.

Brand strategy

We developed a strategy made up of several statements that acted as the building blocks:

We will communicate our vision powerfully – internally and externally worldwide, connecting with our target audiences with a powerful vision and celebrating excellence in marketing and innovation.

↓

We will generate a powerful sense of internal accountability and ownership.

↓

We will create a fully resourced long-term plan and implement it forcefully, attacking key geographic and product markets.

↓

We will seize the emotional high ground in sport – behave like leaders, not followers.

↓

We will continually develop new points of difference and attitude between us and the competition, building the 'in tune' concept of a core competence in our culture.

↓

We will be motivated with winners and winning, attracting and retaining the best people and best players.

↓

Dunlop will inspire a new generation of committed younger sports players.

Embarking on the rejuvenation programme

The customer value proposition: being in tune

For strategic clarity we defined our customer value proposition which we named 'being in tune', reprising our strategy of understanding and reflecting the consumer's needs. The proposition captures the net benefit that a customer derives from using the brand, based on its functional, rational, emotional and relational value delivery.

Rationally 'in tune'

The brand owns 'response technology': cutting-edge innovation equipment that is genuinely responsive to the players' game.

Relationally 'in tune'

The brand is projected through its demonstrably superior understanding of, and commitment to, the physical, mental and emotional game. This involves developing new activity at consumer and trade level.

Functionally 'in tune'

The brand delivers superior quality products, and its presence and visibility is created by excellent marketing, high profile events and association with successful professionals.

Emotionally 'in tune'

People associated with the brand have passion and commitment, and connect directly and continuously with committed young players from grass roots to pro level, supporting and encouraging them.

Ground rules for future success

To enable us to deliver our consumer proposition we set ourselves some ground rules:

Deliver real product benefits

We will ensure we have superior quality product that delivers its promise through cutting-edge technology and research and development. We will exit customers who cannot, or will not, work with us to communicate our message. Already we have developed Abzorber tennis balls, which help prevent tennis elbow, and improved tennis rackets. We have introduced custom squash rackets to offer choice of balance and weight.

Create presence and visibility

We will do this by creating good advertising, associating with a big-name player or celebrity, and associating the brand with successful professionals at high-profile events. We aim to ensure visibility on the professional tour and create an impact by doing something 'big bang'.

Our advertising is directly linked to our 'digging deeper' strategy, with its strapline 'made of the right stuff'. The advertising is bold and arresting, and focuses on the emotional, not the technological benefits of Dunlop. It is consistently used, being carried through to our website and packaging.

Our website identity and imagery mirrors the advertising and has the same feel. Currently we have 20,000 visitors a month and we have constantly striven to make the content interesting and relevant to customers. We intend to make the site more interactive and develop a dialogue with our visitors.

Dare to be different

In future we will not focus on the equipment when talking to consumers, unlike most other equipment manufacturers. We will not copy, but be unique. We will no longer be afraid to link the success of Dunlop tyres in motor sport with our Dunlop brand.

Get connected at grass roots

We will demonstrate our understanding of the emotions of sport. Sampling products will get them into people's hands, and the website is used to offer expert advice to customers.

To encourage word of mouth endorsement, we are investing in

Two advertisements from the current Dunlop series

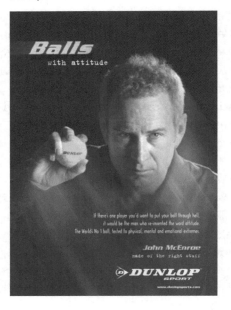

a UK coaching programme and will replicate the learning from this exercise in Germany, France and the United States. We are supporting junior players with real talent. We are implementing a sample programme and upgrading our coaching programme via the web.

Retailers need to be educated to explain the benefits of our products, so we have prepared very comprehensive information packs for them, supported with extensive point of sale material, leaflets and consumer catalogues. They have been very supportive of our efforts and recognize our will to change the brand for the better.

Support young players

Dunlop will help young players turn into good players. Our goal is to support inspiring, exciting, flair players with charismatic personalities who can show their emotions and make a positive statement about the brand. Already the benefits of this strategy are being shown with our support for Thomas Johansson, our first Grand Slam winner for 20 years. We have also supported Mark Philipoussis, Wayne Ferrera, Cedric Pioline, James Blake and Tommy Haas, great players and also great characters. Our supported team is stronger than ever and will be critical to the brand's success.

Create the culture

We need to believe in being the best and be dedicated to achieving it, to be excited, pumped up and feel like a team, united behind the brand. The culture within Dunlop is gradually changing: it helped a lot to have a series of big events announcing the rejuvenation programme. All the individuals in the company attended a presentation so they could experience the new strategy and communication imagery for themselves.

We actively encourage staff to consider themselves Dunlop ambassadors and have consciously attempted to build a team ethic. Spectacular floor to ceiling images of our professional players have been introduced to the offices and ensure that everyone absorbs the brand messages. Our invoices and order forms feature pictures of our players, and our sales messages are now part of the on-hold message on our telephone system.

We are changing our own behaviour: for example, through a greater level of informality in our German office, with Christian names now the norm and a Christmas tree installed for Christmas.

We have held a series of 'Digging Deep' awards to reward our staff and associates who demonstrate the spirit of Dunlop by achievements that go above and beyond the norm. Winners have included Sarah Fitz-Gerald, one of our supported squash players who recovered from serious injury to become world number one.

We have held the first ever conference for licensees of our shoes, and this will now become an annual event. They now use the same promotional materials as the rest of us and have become operationally more synergistic with us. They feel they belong to the Dunlop family.

Moving forward

The programme is still 'work in progress'. We will take our lessons from the UK and from the tennis sector and apply them in the rest of our territories and in the golf sector. We have learned that to effect change you have to focus on your internal resource first, and that you need resilience to finish what you started. Real change is an act of faith, so you have to stick with it.

It is also important for the project manager to have the authority to be able to enforce change if necessary, if people are unwilling to undertake the changes themselves. You need to plan for long-term impact, but take short-term opportunities. You must keep up the momentum by moving quickly and rewarding success.

Communication and information flow has been carefully thought through and executed. All the corporate identity and advertising work has been produced on CDs which are available to each territory. Because so much material is provided, we have found that brand guidelines are not being breached and consistency is maintained.

The fact that the rejuvenation was driven from the top was critical, and it is essential to have a project manager and team who can cut through log jams and force change.

From employees to consumer, brands belong to people. You need to alter behaviour to alter the brand and its chances of success. We have made a good start – our people are now engaged, we have powerful brand images and communications in place – so now we just have to be patient and stay the course.

The editors comment

Brands are not built in a day. And, by the same token, strong brands last and last. However, if they are neglected, they slowly wither, and while they may not die in the popular consciousness, they may acquire unwanted or negative associations which impede progress. Dunlop Sport was certainly such a brand. The famous Dunlop name, so well known in different contexts, had been overtaken by more recent contenders in this most competitive and emotional of markets. The forming of a 'Rejuvenation Team' heralded a deter- mined and holistic approach to breathing new life into the brand. Involving all key functions within the company, this vision-led group of top managers drove change through the entire organization. From the top level down, via the 'action teams' in middle management, to the rest of the company, the new messages were driven home. Feedback from the field returned through the same route, completing a virtuous circle of inclusive brand awareness. Inti- mate, detailed knowledge of customer desires and requirements guided all positioning and competitive considerations. Recognizing the key brand driv- ers, links to leading players, and the games themselves, were strengthened or re-established. All dimensions were thus addressed, and Dunlop Sport is now positioned to take advantage of its renewed brand strength.

Conclusion

The future of brands is inclusive

It is clear, from our knowledge of their history, that brands have come a long way. Therefore it is reasonable to assume that, given the ever-increasing pace of change, they will go a long way further. But in what direction? And at what speed?

One certainty is that, as companies grow (as they must) and the world shrinks, brands must respond to the forces of globalization. This is a process that has been accelerating for decades, but the acceleration has become exponential. The global context demands an inclusive view, because the complexities are such that no simple mechanism can cope with the range of cultural and other market differences, which form barriers to acceptance. It is no longer enough just to brand consistently everywhere. World brands without respect for local conditions may be seen as potentially overpowering, threatening or even exploitative.

We believe that global brands, portrayed as potentially evil and manipulative by some, could actually be a force for good. Because the more brands are conceived and developed in an inclusive way, the more the interests of all stakeholders are taken into account and addressed. Moreover, this trend is already clear in that the openness demanded of corporations, led by analysts, is now vastly greater than it was 20 years ago, in areas such as environmental accountability or employment policies. And these, as we have seen, are key aspects of a holistic brand.

It may be that, in some cases, these 'caring' dimensions of a brand's character have been treated, and consequently viewed by external audiences, with some cynicism. It may be also that certain brands have traded on these dimensions (The Body Shop comes to mind as an example). But the opportunistic positioning of a brand as, say, eco-friendly is not the same as a total positioning that respects the needs and demands of internal and external stakeholders and then weaves this essential strand of attitudes and behaviour through the entire strategy and leadership. As companies take on board this inclusive way of creating and managing brands – essentially becoming brand-led organizations and using brand management as a force for change – then the risks of treating any group of stakeholders (for example, employees) in an unacceptable, unproductive or neglectful way will be much reduced.

However – and it is a big 'however' – brands are there to compete, and to enable their supporting organizations to thrive and prosper. So the need for socially acceptable activities must be balanced against the demands of survival in difficult global conditions. And this is precisely why inclusive branding, through a holistic approach, is the only direction in which brands can move in the future.

The case histories in this book prove this beyond doubt. The actuality, principles, building blocks or potential of holistic branding are present in each and every one. In each case, it is the deployment of all relevant branding resources that has ensured success, and that, in most cases, has been seen as vital, logical, inescapable. The market forces dictate that, as does the absolute internal necessity of aligning everybody behind the brand. But, most of all, there is the pressing need to optimize all of these available resources, so that no chance goes to waste in the battle for profile, differentiation – and survival.

The most successful brands deploy all available resources to create a completely holistic substance and expression. They are focused on, managed according to, and therefore directed by, a vision. All of their activities are coordinated towards achievement of their vision, and towards the inclusion of stakeholders and relationships with customers. In short, these brands have become the driving force in corporate strategic management.

This is where brands are going. The principles of holistic brand management are being translated into the ways in which companies are run. Their potential in change management, for example, is being gradually discovered and harnessed, which must be seen in the context of the importance of, and ever-present need for, change. In addition, all this has serious consequences for corporate structures, which must eventually adapt to brand-led realities in a future environment of increasing interdependencies and complexity.

There is also another dimension of brand management which will count increasingly in future: cost effectiveness. Two principal aspects are material to the costs associated with brands. First, the cost of formal communications has become in some instances prohibitive. Second, it is economically irresponsible to ignore the plethora of other informal channels of communication that encompass all the contacts that people have with brands. Only the holistic approach recognizes and utilizes all of these opportunities for brand expression, and therefore optimizes cost-effectiveness.

There is every reason to believe that, with the word 'holistic' on so many lips, the trend towards inclusive branding will accelerate. With this will arrive the realization that the brand has become the guiding principle in steering the company, that the brand is the foundation for its strategy, and that the brand forms the framework for its organization. The brand will become the primary, decisive corporate asset, managed at the highest level through professional processes. The brand will be valued, and it will be accountable to its stakeholders, its customers and to the wider society. Its standards of behaviour will be audited. In the brand will rest all of the intangible capital of the company, the product, the organization. And on the brand will rest success or failure.

Of course, many enlightened brand owners already take this view of their properties. But too many still treat brands as add-on options, to be dealt with by specialists. Branding is an activity that should involve everybody concerned. Taking an inclusive view ensures ongoing relevance, vitality and competitiveness. It ensures healthy brands. It is the future of brands, as well as of the companies, communities and society that they serve.

Index